LOKA

A JOURNAL FROM NAROPA INSTITUTE
Edited by Rick Fields

Anchor Books   Anchor Press / Doubleday   Garden City, New York

The Anchor Books edition is the first publication of *Loka*.
Anchor Books edition: 1975

ISBN: 0-385-02312-X
Library of Congress Catalog Card Number 74-31515
Copyright © 1975 by Nalanda Foundation / Naropa Institute
All Rights Reserved
Printed in the United States of America
First Edition

"How actually to handle the great challenge . . ."
Chogyam Trungpa

LOKA   A Journal from Naropa Institute

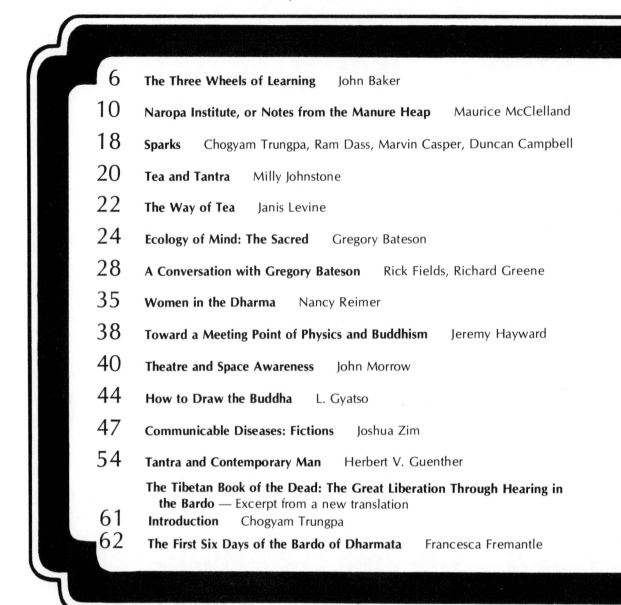

Rick Fields
Editor

David Joel
Managing Editor

Bea Ferrigno
Design/Production

Susan Ross
Art Director/Associate Editor

with help from

Editorial
John Bazzi, Jim Burbank, Juli Clark, Buzz Erikson, Jim Graham, Richard Greene, Elizabeth Harper, Steve Jaffe, Andrew Joel, Julie Runk, Layne Russell, and Peter Stickney.

Art
Cheryl Baer, Bob Del Tredici, Gina Janowitz, Michael Scott, Tara, and Cathy Zimmerman.

Production
Marshall Bishop, David Feig, Martha Margolis, Bob Thompson, and Roger Ben Wilson.

We would like to thank all the authors, artists, photographers, transcribers, typists and designers who contributed their time, energy, and imagination. All LOKA royalties will go to Naropa Institute.

Front cover
calligraphy:
ཨ (LO) ཀ (KA)
Tibetan transliteration
by Chogyam Trungpa.

Back cover: Garuda, the symbol of the awakened state of mind, the celestial hawk of Indian mythology which hatches from its egg fully developed. The Tibetan reads: **Firmly Planting the Victorious Banner of Dharma.**

Frontispiece design by Glen Eddy.

The photograph on page 17 shows the Japanese character *Ho*, which means Dharma.

Designs on pages 70 and 144 by Gina Janowitz.

The illustration on page 101 shows the Sahasrabhuja Avalo-kitesvara mudra.

The articles by Gregory Bateson, Herbert V. Guenther, Allen Ginsberg, Ram Dass and Agehananda Bharati were transcribed and edited from talks given at Naropa Institute, Summer 1974.

LOKA, 1441 Broadway, Boulder, Colorado 80302, is the Journal of Naropa Institute, a division of Nalanda Foundation, a non-profit, educational corporation.

The Three Wheels of Learning

John J. Baker

In the summer of 1974, after a bare nine months of planning, Naropa Institute ran its first ten-week summer session in Boulder, Colorado. That such a significant event could spring to life in so short a time is a source of wonder. The pages of this book are testimony to the enormous success and scope of this event in which more than two thousand students and one hundred faculty participated.

In the summer of 1975 the Institute will re-open a similar session and then, hopefully, in January 1976 will begin its first full academic year. A great deal has occurred in a very short period of time.

The Institute is the product of a long-standing, long-developing American concern with things "Eastern" — most specifically, Buddhism and Hinduism. Naropa Institute was founded by Chogyam Trungpa, Rinpoche, a Tibetan Buddhist lama and meditation master, former Abbot of the Surmang Monasteries in Tibet, who has been teaching Tibetan Buddhist thought and practice in this country since 1970. It was organized and administered by his students. And although it was Eastern religion which attracted many participants, the Institute is not a seminary or church school.

Naropa Institute takes as its model, to some extent, the great Indian institution, Nalanda, which flourished from the fifth through the twelfth centuries A.D. Nalanda was a Buddhist-administered but nonetheless secular institution which provided a focus for almost all areas of learning current in India at the time — religion, philosophy, the sciences, and the arts. In the same spirit, Naropa Institute offers courses ranging from modern American poetry, anthropology, and the history of science to the *Bhagavad Gita,* Buddhist philosophy, and Christian mysticism. However, if any one concern could be identified as dominant, both at Nalanda and at Naropa Institute, it is the concern with the development of the *whole* individual, an approach in which learning is treated not as a process of acquisition, but rather as one of growth, maturation, becoming.

The concern is with the development of a technique of education and a supportive environment in which the processes of learning, discovery, and growth extend from the most minute details of daily life into the classroom and out into the world of affairs. And so the Institute, looking to Nalanda as a model, has taken as the underpinnings of its educational philosophy the traditional Buddhist structure of the Three Wheels of Learning — intellectual study, meditation, and the application of these two to the details of living in the world at large. Although it is somewhat presumptuous in so short a space to attempt a description of such a profound and complex tradition, these terms need some definition.

It is the view at the Institute — and not a new one by any means — that all intellectual systems of description and explanation are both inexorably arbitrary and beautifully necessary constructs. We start with the supposition that the nature of language itself — not to mention political, religious, philosophical, and psychological systems of thought — provides the interpretive scenarios out of which we formulate our many and varied worlds. These constructs are, on the positive side, the means by which we express our creativity, and on the negative side, the expressions of our narrow-mindedness, self-centeredness, and self-imprisonment. Ironically, perhaps, it is by immersing oneself in a particular discipline and mastering it thoroughly that the student may transcend its limits. By becoming an expert in a particular view, the student, hopefully, is equipped to see its limitations and also to use that view with compassion, grace, and skill. Thus the first wheel, study, demands both mastery and skepticism.

But the views by which we both apprehend and delimit our worlds are more than purely intellectual, and so the second wheel — meditation. The Eastern forms of "meditation" have been largely misrepresented and misunderstood in the West, for they are more than mental gymnastics or techniques for calming the mind. Meditation, though it may start with a particular technique, is ultimately a path to or a way of being, involving clear and accurate perception of life as it is, beyond the limits of personal intellectual or emotional interpretation. Not that intellect or the emotions are to be rejected. Rather they are to be liberated from the role of tools for self-protection or self-aggrandizement. Intellect and emotion then may be used as powerful and creative forms of communication. The techniques of meditation are many and varied, but they all have a common theme — direct perception of the object of meditation without comment, judgment or interpretive mental remarks.

The type of education described in the two wheels of study and meditation is aimed not at producing a person who is identified as a "psychologist," "artist," or whatever. Rather it is aimed at producing a skilled and disciplined person who knows himself to be a citizen of the world, or of the universe, for that matter, a human being in the most fundamental sense. Such an education can only be "learned" or "taught" in the beginning, and then it must be lived. The techniques of study and meditation — intellectual mastery, skepticism, direct contact, openness, and involvement — must become a part of the individual's lived experience.

We might call the third wheel "skillful action" or "total and intelligent involvement in life." It seems improbable that one person can ever teach another how to live sanely and creatively. But it might be possible for one to open a door, point a finger, make a suggestion, and in so doing help another to discover his or her own individual uniqueness and complexity. The ways in which the Institute can "point a finger" are subtle in quality, infinite in number, and difficult to effect. However, there are certain steps which may be taken as part of the third wheel: the creation of a community-based style of education, a community of teachers, students, and administrators who share a common inspiration, and a faculty who regard themselves as students as well as teachers.

The Institute has set itself a difficult task — starting from scratch to create a university. But judging from the response to the first summer session, the need and desire for this approach to education are strong. There is a great deal of work to be done — putting together a flexible curriculum, experimenting with different types of evaluative criteria, developing a more efficient but un-entrenched administrative organization, and of course, coping with the ever-present and always difficult money problems. But everyone seems to view the project as a labor of love. As Gregory Bateson has said of the students at Naropa's first session, ". . . it is not uncommon to find people willing to work hard, but it is unusual to find people who really care."

I think everyone involved in the Institute has found the experience exciting, rewarding, and disconcerting. Perhaps this is because we are not trying to pacify or integrate the extremes — mind and body, intuition and intellect, the sciences and the arts, East and West. Rather we are attempting to provide an open space in which the extremes may meet and spark. As Chogyam Trungpa remarked in his opening address to the Institute, "We are making hot chili." So be it.

John J. Baker is a vice-president of Naropa Institute

LOKA means space, place, realm in Sanskrit, and is the root word for local, locus. The particular world this LOKA represents is the world of Naropa Institute, summer 1974, Boulder, Colorado. The Naropa Loka is an intense realm somewhere right in the middle of it all, up against the foothills of the Rockies, between east and west.

LOKA began halfway through the summer as a workshop called *The Magazine Project.* **So much was going on it seemed worthwhile to catch a glimpse of it in print. LOKA is a record in which a community of scholars, artists, and meditators argue, hold forth, discuss, keep silent, paint.**

Naropa's premise is that clear hard thinking is central to a sane spiritual journey; that what is needed is a crossroads where the intellectual-critical mind and the way of experience and meditation meet head-on, and open to each other.

No longer, it seems, do we feel that the way is best found by turning back nostalgically to what we imagined the "East" to be. In fact, there is no turning back; this vehicle has no reverse. There is just the place we live, worlds spinning around us, and the work we do there.

— Rick Fields

Naropa, great siddha and pandit of Nalanda University

Drawing by Glen Eddy

Everything in LOKA was either spoken, written, overheard, drawn, photographed or thought by faculty/students/visitors at Naropa Institute.

Maurice McClelland, who wrote the definitive letter home on page 10, is Associate Director of the International Theatre Institute. He created theatre events at the Museum of Modern Art and the Main Cathedral in Antwerp, Belgium. **Milly Johnstone** studied at the Urasenke School of Tea in Tokyo and Kyoto. She writes for the *Chanoyu Quarterly*, and was one of the founders of the Urasenke School in New York. Her assistant at Naropa, **Janis Levine**, studied Tea for two years in Kyoto. **Gregory Bateson**, originator of the double-bind theory of schizophrenia, and author of *Balinese Character* and *Steps to an Ecology of Mind*, taught a course on "The Evolutionary Idea" at Naropa, and is currently writing a book on the same subject. **Nancy Reimer** lives in a small community in the East Bay Redwoods, where she runs a nursery school.

Jeremy Hayward, a vice-president of Naropa Institute, has spent four years at Karme Choling (formerly Tail of the Tiger), a Buddhist meditation community in Vermont. He holds a Ph.D. in Nuclear Physics from Cambridge University. **John Morrow**, who taught "Collaborations in Space" with Maurice McClelland, has written, acted and directed at La Mama and Theater Genesis.

L. Gyatso was born in Lhasa, Tibet. He studied thangka painting in Dharamsala, and at the Sakya Monastery in Dehra Dun, India, and also Art and Economics at the Claverhan Country School in England. The Drawings for "How to Draw the Buddha" were done by a student in Thangka I. **Joshua Zim** was the coordinator of Lama Foundation in New Mexico before getting lost in Boulder, where he is suffering from *Com-*

municable Diseases. **Herbert V. Guenther** has translated, with commentary, *The Life and Teachings of Naropa*, and *The Jewel Ornament of Liberation*, and is the author of *The Tantric View of Life*. He holds Ph.D. degrees from the Universities of Munich and Vienna, and was Head of the Department of Buddhist Studies at the Sanskrit University in Varanasi, India. He is currently Head of the Department of Far Eastern Studies at the University of Saskatchewan. Dr. Guenther taught a course on "The History of the Kagyupa School," and climbed several mountains while at Naropa. **Francesca Fremantle** holds a Ph.D. in Sanskrit from the University of London. She has translated *The Guhyasamaja Tantra*, as well as *The Great Liberation Through Hearing In The Bardo*. Dr. Fremantle taught a Naropa course in "Tantric Literature."

Allen Ginsberg has been building a cabin in Northern California. His major collection *The Fall of America* is published by City Lights. *Allen Verbatim: Lectures On Poetry, Politics, and Consciousness* is a book which records talks and conversations during a cross country reading tour. **John Cage**, composer, poet, and essayist, studied with D.T. Suzuki at Columbia in the fifties. During his weekend visit to Naropa he found time to pick and cook local mushrooms. **Ram Dass** taught psychology at Harvard, researched psychedelics with Timothy Leary, and studied under the Indian Master, Neem Karoli Baba. He has recently formed the Hanuman Foundation to help support meditation and retreat centers, and to bring qualified teachers to this country.

Richard Greene ran the Whole Earth Store in Evanston, Illinois. **Deborah Katz** studied ballet at The American School of Dance, and Indian Dance with Sujata Rabiner. **Arlyn Ray** spent more than two years in India studying Indian classical dance (Odissi style) with Guru Surendranath Jana. **Judyth Weaver** studied modern dance with Martha Graham. For the last five years she has practiced T'ai Ch'i Ch'uan under the direction of Professor Ching Man-Cheng. **Ben Weaver**, former director of Esalen Institute, studied Sensory Awareness with Charlotte Selver. He has also worked on aid programs in Nepal and Vietnam. **Duncan Campbell** practices law in Denver, and is the moderator of Naropa's "Open Secret" radio series.

Ives Waldo has taught karate, kendo, and sitar. He received a Ph.D. in philosophy from the University of Kansas. **Robert Newman**, an Associate Professor at City University of New York, is completing a full-length study of the Lohan statues. **Sunno Bhikku** (Jack Kornfield) has lived as a Buddhist monk in Thai, Lao, and Burmese monasteries. He is currently working towards a Ph.D. in meditation and psychology at the Humanistic Psychology Institute. **Agehananda Bharati** studied at the University of Vienna, and the Dashanami Samnyasi Mahavidyalaya in Varanasi, India. He has traveled the length of India on foot as a Hindu monk, and is currently Chairman of the Department of Anthropology at Syracuse University. He is the author of an autobiography, *The Ochre Robe*, as well as *The Tantric Tradition*, and *Asians in East Africa*. He is currently writing a book on the Hindu and Buddhist Tantras. **Chogyam Trungpa**, Rinpoche, is a meditation master in the Kargyu and Nyingma schools of Tibetan Buddhism. He was abbot of the Surmang monasteries in Tibet until he emigrated to India. He subsequently studied comparative religion, psychology, and art at Oxford University. Since 1970 he has lived in the United States, where he has taught Buddhist meditation, philosophy, and practice. His books include *Born in Tibet, Meditation In Action, Mudra, Cutting Through Spiritual Materialism*, and *The Myth of Freedom*. He is the founder and president of Naropa Institute.

POETRY: All the poets in LOKA traveled through or stayed put at Naropa. **Allen Ginsberg** and **Chogyam Trungpa** spoke their linked-verse poem into a tape-recorder without premeditation. **Anne Waldman** has worked for ten years with The Poetry Project in New York. City Lights is publishing the complete *Fast Speaking Woman* as Pocket Poets # 33. **Sidney Goldfarb** heads the writing program at the University of Colorado, and lives in a cabin above Salina. His book, *Messages*, is published by Noonday. **Jackson MacLow**, a pioneer of "chance operation" poetry, studied with D.T. Suzuki and John Cage. *Stanzas For Iris Lezak* is published by Something Else Press. **Alex, Mini,** and **Diane DiPrima** live and write together on the California coast. Diane DiPrima was an early student of

Suzuki Roshi. Part I of her long poem *Loba* is published by Capra Press. **Jim Burbank** lives in Boulder where he edits *LOS*. Part V of his book-length poem *Lines* appears in *The Active Anthology*. **John Giorno**, who produced the original "Dial-A-Poem" and a record "Dial-A-Poem Disconnected," is the author of *Balling Buddha* (Kulchur), and *Cancer In My Left Ball* (Something Else Press). **Sara Vogeler** has published in *Io* and *The Rocky Mountain Review*. **Rick Fields** has written on "Applepicking" and "Beginning Buddhism" for *The Whole Earth Epilog* and *The CoEvolution Quarterly*. **Lewis MacAdams** helped plan a community-controlled water system for Bolinas, California. *The Poetry Room* is published by Harper & Row. **George Quasha** is the editor of *America A Prophecy* (Random House), and *The Active Anthology* (Sumac). His long poem, *Somapoetics*, is published by Sumac.

LOKATIONS: David Joel, managing editor of LOKA, taught a Naropa course on the novels of Herman Hesse, and paints sometimes. **Victoria Thompson** is a nurses's aide and a student of Chinese painting. **Enid Goldstein** was a student at Naropa. **Johanna Demetrakas** directed the film *Womanhouse*. **Brother John Doyle**, professor of Religious Studies at Iona College, is a member of the Congregation of Christian Brothers. **Miriam** and **Jose Arguelles** are the authors of *Mandala*. **Diane Ames** is continuing her Tibetan language studies. **Marvin Casper** taught a Naropa course on "The Politics of Transcendence in America." He was co-editor (along with **John Baker**) of *Cutting Through Spiritual Materialism*. **Anne Jurika** designs mandalas with colored string. **Dr. Thich Thien-An**, a professor at the University of Saigon and Van-Hanh Buddhist University, is head of the International Buddhist Meditation Center, and President of the College of Oriental Studies in Los Angeles. He has written *The Zen-Pure Land Union in Modern Vietnamese Buddhism*.

Susan Ross was an illustrator for Lama Foundation's *Be Here Now*, and is a roving consultant for the Polaroid Corporation. **Bea Ferrigno** enjoys gardening and does printing design. Her free-lance work includes *Garuda III*. **Eugene Gregan** received an M.F.A. from the Yale School of Fine Arts. He lives and paints on a farm in New York State.

NAROPA INSTITUTE

Photo courtesy of Friends of Naropa

Photo by Bob Del Tredici

Chogyam Trungpa, Rinpoche

or,

Notes from the

Manure Heap

Boulder, Colorado
Summer 1974

Dear Robert:

First you should know something about how I got here. A year and a half ago, when Jean-Claude Van Itallie asked me to help him get together a theatre conference in Boulder, I said yes because I had met Chogyam Trungpa, Rinpoche, just a week earlier (on my birthday) in Bob Wilson's loft, and we did it. There were 40 theatre experimenters gathered from around the country to meet with him and 40 others, mostly his students, but including Sufi dancers and so on. At the end of the week Rinpoche said that what had been shown was extremely complicated and seemed to leave a gap between the performer, reality, and the performance, because all the physical work was being taught onto the already neurotic bodies of the performers as something additional. He said that there was no way to orient one's body in space in motion with complete awareness of what it was doing. So he took two days to teach us some exercises designed to offend space so that space would mind our bodies' business.

You know what a garbage bucket my mind is, but from that week of teaching, which seemed to be incredibly basic and simple, and from a few scattered meetings later, without apparent content, I began to really think about space as my ego's counterpart — and as something I might be able to work with, finding my ego to be intractable, slippery and increasingly tiresome.

So when I took Peter Brook to meet Rin-poche at Jean-Claude's house in Charlemont, he said that he was starting Naropa Institute and asked all of us whether or not we would come and teach about theatre. I said yes immediately, disclaiming all ability beyond interest to do it, Jean-Claude said he would have to think about it, and Peter Brook went to bed to rest from their conversation. So I knew all along I would be doing it, but not how to describe what I wanted to do. It seemed to be something without "theatre background" and only about space and one night I realized that if I could find John Morrow, who did a piece with me for the University Without Walls and who was in *Ritual Worlds from Space* for me at the Museum of Modern Art, that we would know together what to do. But he was off in the mountains, living in a teepee. Next morning walking from my funky new 22nd Street loft to the subway, there was John climbing out of the subway I was headed into and before I could get my mouth open, he said, "Listen, did you hear about that thing called Naropa Institute — how can we get there?" "Easy," I said. Well it wasn't that easy, but we wrote a proposal to them for a course overlapping the two 5-week sessions for two weeks on each side, called *Collaborations in Space*, and we got here; John, Christina, and their 14-month-old visitor, Casey, traveling in a big yellow school bus with their teepee on top. Naropa had rented a campground for the thousands of penniless groupies who threatened everybody's worst dreams, but who never arrived, and they put me in a sort of Howard

Johnson stage-set apartment where there are two bathrooms, a garbage disposal and a dishwasher, with a roommate who teaches about Hesse, reminds me a lot of you, and is the other faculty member here who is an underground theist, amidst chaotic misunderstanding and quite a lot of real teaching about Buddhism. It was all put together so fast that most of the accidents are terrifyingly "right."

During the first session Ram Dass was here being the alternative energy, with about 800 of his "followers," most of whom had only read one of his books, never met him, and came from Texas, Alabama, Oklahoma, and Georgia to Naropa because after buying his book they got a flyer in the mail about it and somehow scraped together the $55 per class tuition plus expenses and got here with no plan for eating during the next five weeks. Somehow that never got to be a problem. Rinpoche's cracks about self-appointed teachers and charlatan poets contrasted nicely with Ram Dass's openness, decorative intelligence, and his apparent love for Rinpoche, which went so far that he ONLY gave his students mantras that did not directly mention the name of any God(s).

The peak of the Ram Dass trip was a full moon all-night chant to Shiva. There were one thousand of us earthlings in a field alongside a housing development on the edge of Boulder, where five port-johns had been set up and two sound trucks from which the over-miked mantra began to rise, sung by Bhagavan Das and others, and answered by our un-miked, not completely convinced voices. So there was this piercing amplified mantra rising over the housing development at a really huge, wet, pulsing white moon — beyond surprise — and our feeble rejoinder, particularly since almost nobody knew what the words we were supposed to be chanting meant. They weren't translated, we were just told they were "powerful," and that by morning we should notice some kind of change. It didn't take that long because Christina, another Capricorn, went over and told Ram Dass to un-

Photo by Tom Raper

plug the speakers that were drowning out the response. He looked surprised, then AGREED and did it. Hard to imagine not planning that kind of production RIGHT. Harder to imagine agreeing that it would be better another way in midcommitment, harder still to imagine smiling and giving off gratitude about it. Well all of that is him. And then the chant got better and I went off to sleep to the music in the back of the school bus, which didn't wait until morning to leave.

Our first class began to work from their own dreams — to dream about the group and its work, to bring their dreams to the group and then have the group work with the dreams. The method of "re-dreaming" certain material and then working with it aggressively during dreaming came from a Malaysian tribe of Indians who share their lives and work and the responsibility for helping each other during difficult dreams. The method of making dreams come to life for each other came from the Hopis. This was happening within a context of exercises on spatial awareness from our limited understanding of Buddhist concepts, but without explaining the background to the students. It led to an amazingly strong ability to work as a group from the beginning to the end of the two-hour period, often without instruction during the class, simply sharing the development and consciousness that existed and risking the direction. We did one public piece in a super-market called KING SOOPER, where people are dislocated into next week's possible menus, and where after more than an hour of complicated trips, nobody knew "a piece" was happening.

Photo by Gary Allen

Photo by Allen Klein

The environment is other teachers, students, teachers as students and the teachings themselves, along with seemingly endless intentional entertainments and meetings — incredibly rich in the summer of a college town that would otherwise seem nearly deserted. But there is also Karma Dzong (action fortress), Rinpoche's meditation community in Boulder which, since he lives here, is the fiercest and most competitive and possibly the least friendly Buddhist community in America. They are not unfriendly either. Just fiercely on their own trip, which means getting hold of him as often as possible in the least shared manner that can be arranged. Which trip they also struggle diligently to avoid. It is, "if I may use such words, 'beautiful' " (a quote from Rinpoche's lecture on the mandala display of our own anger, lust and greed, which took place as part of his class on meditation, attended last session by over 1,000 people three times a week). So between Naropa Institute which grew out of it, and Karma Dzong, the local Buddhists are owning a lot of real estate and renting a lot more. And there is still plenty of outdated wonderfully large institutional architecture to acquire, since it's a college town, and they are busily about that too. In their own downtown headquarters there seems to be a new culture developing like a bubble inside the corpse of the old one. The building is beautifully painted inside with white walls and bright orange-red and yellow and sky-blue trimming over the turn-of-the-century wood-work. The meditation hall is so perfectly Tibetan-American that when I first attempted sitting there I just tripped out instead on what the Gyalwa Karmapa will see when he comes

here in September and discovers this Tibetan-American living, design, acquisition, teaching, and planting of long, long roots. It made me really happy to think about that reaction. I read later that he is coming to give the "black hat ceremony," which blew my mind still a little further away.

People throw up a lot here at parties. There seem to be very few people empty enough to absorb a fraction of what is going on. The tendency is for people in the second session to switch from a schedule that included Herbert Guenther, Rinpoche, Ram Dass, etc., etc., in the first session, to one sensory awareness class or just Rinpoche's course in Tantra. The second session was a real shock. Ram Dass left; the bearded, white-clothed moly-bead-counters packed up their love and light and flew off; in marched the Zen folk with their black zafus or wooden meditation seats under one arm, and a lean and hungry, very serious mien. (Our first class found touching each other an extremely unpleasant necessity.) And among this group, there's this smiling giant, Gregory Bateson, who started the Palo Alto schizophrenia project, and whom I will finally hear tonight, and a frail American woman named Millie Johnstone, who my Japanese soul-sister Kazuko says does a heavy tea ceremony — and when I told her I brought her greetings from Kazuko, the formal tea manner exploded into a hug and TWO kisses.

And in this session our class begins with the theme of death — we start each session with a "dance" where we carry our own deaths in our stomachs and let them teach us to move with them. Who knows, it could go from there into birth or transformation, but we are trying to

Photo by Ludwig Turzanski

teach the LITERAL content of Buddhist space concepts this time, so Insha'ah Allah!

Fucking is the subtext for all action outside the classes which are too absorbing to get completely supplanted. And walking every night into a room of 1,200 people or so, most of them as interesting as your best friends and at least half of whom are more beautiful-seeming than any other given segment of the population, and whose average age is about fifteen years younger than my 37 years, is a complicated subtext to the subtext of fucking. When I sat atop one of the very high slopes of rock the earth has thrown up here, called "flatirons," I looked across town and experienced that subtext as overhanging the place, lower but as palpable as the mountains and, from that "God-like" perspective, became aware that it is a subtext because in all likelihood as I gazed across the roof of each house and car and motel at 3:17 on a Sunday afternoon, no fucking was going on. Nevertheless, I frequently interview the two most hungry-looking exceptions to that rule, indiscriminately affectionate guys dressed in cutoffs and suntans, and they have excellent reports ranging almost daily from 15-year-old groupies to small friendly crowds. As for myself these interviews are only to put into perspective the display of my own mandala, which includes the worst case of acne since adolescence and a stance

about three leaps backward from involvement, from the numerous people my wolfie instincts are struggling to keep me "in love with" and at which entire subtext I alternately laugh and cry. Tequila, wine, beer, and ouzo seem to be the general medicine against this all too common complaint, the last being the one I favor most since we had each other before in a time that corresponds with my current case of acne.

Rinpoche has the *chutzpah* to call all this the demonstration of our personal mandala display and something he encourages like any other manure heap or fertilization for tender, hungry growing things. Last night in his class on Tantra, he described three coexisting mandala forms in us:

The External, relating to politics, domesticity, the world of interconnections, relationships;

The Internal, bodily awareness and the sense of reality — a sense of confidence that the way we were taught manners usually interferes with, but is based upon, intention, reality and discovery; and

The Secret (or sacred) realm of psychological, meditative behavior, corresponding on one level to the world of the emotions, where we need to cultivate awareness, openness, and NO HESITATION to deal in the moment's situation with one's own emotions. He said that if we could get into a space where our meditative consciousness would let us look at these parts of our own mandala, we would find this connection: Passion leading to aggression, leading to ignorance, leading to jealousy and envy, with the circle also connected from front to back as well. We could regard ALL emotions "as big deal," because they all exist in our minds and are all the same problem, which is the seed of something workable. Naturally somebody asked him how to do it, and he replied, "It's a REAL experience. There's no HOW to do it, you did it already, that's where your chance is, you've manifested the secret mandala already." When somebody else asked an even less useful question, he said so, adding, "Good luck, sir."

You are wondering how a sieve-like mind has retained so much from one half-hour talk. What happens when we aren't struggling with what to bring into our own classes is that people fall by and cook huge meals together, rapping endlessly about what this one or that one said in such and such a talk and whether or not any of it is workable in any context and whether or not a context is still lurking out there — interruptions for news flashes from somebody who's seen a paper or TV — about new violence, deaths, and the progress of impeachment. And there are a whole lot of these efficiency stage sets all over the little town, some with swimming pools and saunas so that the mind multiplies these meetings of the elders of Jerusalem in Babylon to dizzying proportions.

So that Gregory Bateson took over from Rinpoche's talk tonight with the "local image of mandalas" and described "The Ecology of Mind," calling love the glue that can stick the two halves (prosaic and abstract) of the brain together and calling the integrations or bridging the vulnerable, explosive, sacred territory. He has so much humor and humanity. But it seemed strange to hear him talk in a friendly way about his "schizophrenic friends" and never hear any clinical news about the biggest reality for them of all — one that obliterates all the others — the reality of involuntary confinement — this country's best answer to everything and the shadow of the search for liberation — a reality that is almost big enough to overshadow death as well as life since death, through graveside services, square holes in the ground, boxes for bodies, has been made into the ultimate form of confinement. And as background for what is happening here it seems strangely appropriate — we should be seeing Cindy Firestone's ATTICA film, not ONLY going to rock dances at night. We should be relating much more to the local Chicanos, six of whom were killed this summer in mysterious bomb blasts, the investigation of which subpoenaed sixty people, ALL Chicanos. So that freedom and its shadow-face get much sharper as a focus than the love and light crew would tell us — more like Rinpoche's scariest talks on Tantra as "the thread of one's life," where he waves his centuries-old Dorje around like some kind of reverse lightning rod. And there are those who would say this freedom-confinement equation is a direct and quantitative relationship, so that the more people there are here doing this, the more others are suffering. Or there is the Buddhist idea, on the other hand, that each person

who becomes a Bodhisattva drags thousands of souls along behind.

But Naropa is also merely an "educational" institution and, even though one of the Ram Dass people from our class moved into Karma Dzong's townhouse to live and learn about Buddhism, and two other young guys came on their last day before returning to Oklahoma to ask me about a path that I happen to have traveled on and that nobody else would have been likely to know about, the incidence of Bodhisattva-making does not seem generally higher than, say, the Lower East Side of New York. And certainly not high enough to justify the extremely low incidence of blacks, latin-afros, or red-skinned people participating (I have seen two blacks amongst us). And with Pir Vilayat Khan coming next week and Swami Muktananda the week following, and Chino Sensei from Japan and two Tibetan lamas in addition to Rinpoche, the high percentage of yellow and brown teachers for all us honkies seems ironic. And, as Bateson pointed out, you can't

manufacture glue in the lefthand (prosaic/manipulative) half of the brain that the right side will stick to. The integration has more to do with what Diane Di Prima told a reporter years ago when he asked her about communism: "It doesn't go nearly far enough. We have to learn to love each other." She comes tomorrow and I am already affected by her vision of this in advance and curious about what it will be in reality.

So there are lots of influences fluencing here — yesterday morning after writing that last paragraph about ethnic minorities I went over to the big lecture hall to tape some music for our class and this technician who acts like it's a PLEASURE to do all kinds of impossible work for us was showing some video tapes of Ram Dass, Rinpoche and others talking about the same problems. And today there is the impossible choice between a tea ceremony being given for Chino Sensei and a film of Jung being interviewed about his own work. And later a concert of dance and electronic music by Alden Jenks, then a poetry reading, *The Dawn Of Tantra*, by Diane Di Prima, Allen Ginsberg and Anne Waldman, who all teach here. Only the threat of having to PRODUCE for and with our students and for and with the other teachers keeps this place from turning into an institutionalized spiritual Woodstock. Its future seems to include accreditation and *degree programs* in Buddhist studies, East-West psychology, and an art school.

There's a lot of excitement and some genuine interest in experimenting with how Buddhist concepts turn art processes upside down. A well-known expressionist painter here said that formerly when she painted, the act itself was one that was neurotic (capturing the feeling of the moment and monumentalizing it) and the process of doing it was compulsive (morning to midnight ceaselessly) and the paintings (which were very popular in art circles) were ABOUT neuroticism. Now she lets the event happen, finds its calm centered colors in her meditation and paints what ALREADY HAPPENED as exactly and as objectively as possible so that the moment "happens" when the painting is looked at — it is a present, not a past, piece of work. This is what we are working toward with our "theatre workshops" — exactly upside down from the idea of "expressing oneself," and a way we are finding to be rich and demanding and satisfying for us in our own lives, too. One of the students in another theatre workshop, taught by Lee Worley, wrote this poem, which became the basis of their theatre piece:

Photo by Susan Ross

. . . This is the story of a mountain who grew up to be a grain of sand.

I am affronted by my ordinariness; angered by my lack of specialness; by my feeling of outsideness; by the choices I face.

I am confused by my situation: by what I know and by what I don't. And, surely, by what it is I'm after.

Body . . . is coterminous with mind.

Life . . . is the ultimate standard of value. Existence is marked by suffering, impermanence and insubstantiality. There is permanence in change. Continuity in discontinuity. There is only to feel as we feel — fearlessly.

Dharma is the path. Experience is just itself. The ordinary is sacred the sacred is ordinary. No mind no garbage: nothing left behind. Nothing else but trust in the Buddha (me) the dharma (it) and the sangha (you).

I. I am. I am here. I am too frail to stand alone. Yet I am the hero of my own life. We are the heroes of our own lives. In our own times.

Well, you can juggle my dhatus, sort my ayatanas, and shuffle my skandhas. I just sit and breathe. Like a gate, opening and closing in the wind. Watching myself disappear —

(when I grow up I want to be
a no body sattva)

Steve Krugman
Naropa Institute 1974

I send you all these words and go back to the air bubble inside the body of the corpse,

Maurice McClelland

Photo by Chögam Trungpa

SPARKS

Photo by Michael Scott

Marvin Casper

Ram Dass

Chogyam Trungpa

Duncan Campbell, moderator

Marvin Casper: I think what we are trying to do with Naropa is not to create a Buddhist university, but more an atmosphere that acknowledges the basic problems of spiritual materialism and meditation. To bring in traditions selectively insofar as they have the spirit of meditation, and a sensitivity to the issue of spiritual materialism. And it is not so much a sectarian thing of which tradition is followed, but more what spirit was the tradition practiced in, expounded, lived?

Ram Dass: But it still feels to me as someone teaching a Hindu tradition course here that this is an alien course to the general framework of Naropa. It doesn't feel to me a totally integrated situation yet.

Chogyam Trungpa: There is a particular philosophy of Naropa which is not so much trying to bring it together, like a spoon of sugar in your lemonade so that it becomes more drinkable, but the point is more like a firework — not so much that each will fight with each other in the destructive sense, but that there is an enormous individualism in terms of the doctrines and teachings that are presented. All of them are valid but at the same time there is a meeting point which takes place in a spark!

RD: I enjoy the spark but you can create a field in which there can be an equal number of contestants coming together to spark. I mean why go into a Buddhist field to spark? The spark can be just where we come together, like you and I come together to do our dance, and that's the spark.

CT: I think it is the same thing actually. Someone has to have some background somewhere. We can say why can't we do this in the Naropa ship going to the moon?

RD: Are we?

CT: But we've got to have it somewhere. We are doing it in the United States.

RD: Yes . . .

CT: In Boulder, Colorado . . . do you remember?

RD: Yes, if I take a stretch I can remember! There are two phenomena that have happened: one, there is the Towards the One concept — which I think is a little premature and uncooked — which is to bring everybody together, and we'll all love each other, and it will become an amalgam. That's putting the sugar in with the lemonade, and it is all palatable and sweet but nothing much is happening. It's all very nice but it lacks the spark. But there is another way, a kind of arena, a fully collaborative arena to have the dialogue in. I am wondering is that possible in America yet? Or do I have to go visit a Buddhist center, and then go fight with Yogi Bhajan then go fight with Suzuki Roshi? I just go out and fight, I'm a free-lance fighter! But there's no place where we can all come into an arena together, all share putting up the money, share taking the losses, share the dormitories, share the administration, share the dynamics. Are we ready for that kind of collaborative sparking?

CT: I don't think we are talking in that sense. I think we are talking in the experiential sense, like eating Mexican food which has lots of chili in it. If you are somewhat hesitant before you eat it, and you ask the waitress how it is, probably the waitress will say, "Oh, it is okay." Then when you eat you have the experience of Mexican food, and that is personal experience. Rather than debating with the chef and the cook about how it should be cooking, which is externalizing and debating the whole thing in the wrong way. It's how sparked this place is in everybody's mind. All the students taking cross-cultural courses of all kinds — the spark is taking place in them which makes them think twice. There is energy happening rather than completion. That's an internal spark we are talking about rather than our having to institute a sort of Dharma game.

RD: Like Naropa Institute — which you just did by creating Naropa Institute.

MC: Well, if I may paraphrase, it isn't Buddhism that's the point, it's the gap between Buddhism or Hinduism or whatever, that creates the spark. It's juxtaposing the systems to go beyond them. I can see that there is a more heavily Buddhist system here in a sense, but creation or solidification of the Buddhist system is not the point, the point is to cut through systems.

RD: And I am saying that cutting through systems can be designed into the institution, as well as our saying inside, "Well, we know it's a Buddhist center, but we really know that it's not really a Buddhist center."

CT: I think the point is that we honor people's experiences and their intellect so that they can conduct their own warfare within themselves while being sharp scholars in language studies, or T'ai Ch'i, or whatever. We don't teach them how to conduct skeptical search.

RD: Right. We don't teach Battle I, II. We assume they know how to do it.

CT: Because the situation is created already, there is pressure, there is enormous energy, there is internal experience.

Duncan Campbell: Well, it almost sounds like the way that you were talking about the hot chili, and the representation of Naropa Institute — it is saying that there are no answers. That no one is going to find an easy way to relate to himself and his own experience, but there is going to be that constant interaction, that spark, the flame between the intellect and intuition, between one tradition and another tradition, one culture and another culture, and that each one of us has to experience that. If it's not being experienced, nothing is happening.

MC: Right. One could look at any tradition as a trap, and say that the purpose of the tradition is to build into itself an escape from its own tradition. And a tradition is good only to the extent that it provides the mechanisms by which you escape from it. Or by which you escape from cruder versions of it to more subtle versions beyond, to breaking through the systematization of it so that the idea of juxtaposing systems, and of juxtaposing intellect and meditation, creates an opportunity to further spark that kind of process.

RD: Escape or entrapment?

MC: Escape.

RD: The predicament is that you don't want to escape until you've been entrapped.

CT: I think that's the point actually. Tradition provides you right in the beginning with a good setting, and provides food, home, shelter, companionship, and someone to look up to, so you can copy his style, her style, whatever. Then at a certain point you begin to discover your own inadequacy. You begin to feel like you're sinking down into the ground, you begin to find that tradition is entrapment, imprisonment. Then you begin to look at it twice, thrice, and find out more about it. Why are you imprisoned? Is it because the tradition is inadequate? That you are such a smart person?

RD: Or has your stance towards the tradition been inadequate?

CT: And then there is a strong possibility of a changing shift which creates a spark. And then again tradition comes back, but instead of being a jail, as a temple, a monastery, or a zendo. It's rediscovering one's imprisonment as a sacredness of some kind . . .

Tea and Tantra

Touch, taste, sight, sound, smell: this is the
    Tea Ceremony, a way to go beyond the senses
    into the world of Being. Tea and Tantra go together —
    invisible moveable patterns — changing, weaving life
    into a tapestry of human design.

Tea flows and keeps flowing. No pot, no spout, no lid —
    just a dipper that keeps pouring and a bowl that
    turns 'round and 'round. Offering, receiving, whisking
    the tea into a jade green froth — froth on the tea
    like the things of this world: fleeting.

Bowing in, bowing out, bending and sitting still.
    Tea Ceremony is a form of meditation, a formal way
    of coming in touch with ourselves and each other,
    no matter who we are or where we came from —
    meditation in action.

Tea and Tantra: involved with tiny gestures that
    grow big, with steps that go far. Odd people
    are our guests and we're odd too. Not knowing
    who we are, strange things happen. We go to
    odd places and meet odd people — all dancing
    the same dance.

Tea Ceremony is a journey into ourselves — in and
    out again. We travel alone with others also alone.
    We bow, we bend. Bowing "In Tea" is not just
    a matter of politeness. It is a way of yielding
    to the mystery of being human.

Milly Johnstone

The Way of Tea

Janis Levine

The art of Tea is a game which plays with the senses while disciplining the body. It arouses aesthetic awareness while calming the wild horses of our minds. Tea is also a Way, a way of regulating our breath while moving through life.

Life itself is a continuum of moments which lead us from our childhood and youth towards old age and death. When we enter upon the Way of Tea, we are taught to move through this continuum, " . . . stirring no dust . . . leaving no traces . . . "

The everyday world in which we are obliged to fulfill our duties is a composite of ups and downs, likes and dislikes. Today we are living a comedy, tomorrow a tragedy. Meditation can become the key which resolves countless perplexities by opening endless dimensions. We sit in a quiet room, breathe in the incense and become one with a certain pervading stillness. Then suddenly, the bell rings and we stand up to leave the meditation hall. How do we act when we re-enter our daily lives: eating, how do we slice the bread? Are we still with it, breathing calmly, deeply, in and out? Some fortunate beings find no difficulty transferring this oneness into their everyday lives, but for most people, it is no easy matter. We are constantly faced with the problem of actualizing what has been realized during meditation.

Some five hundred years ago, in Japan, a man named Sen-no-Rikyu was faced with this dilemma. Because his family were merchants, he was brought up to view life practically. However, he was also a man deeply in touch with himself through his practice of zazen, Zen sitting meditation. Rikyu sought a way to join together his Zazen Mind and his everyday mind. His final solution was "Cha-no-yu" — "hot water for tea" — or as it is translated into English, "Tea Ceremony." Rikyu skillfully wove together the various strands of the art of Tea which had been developing in Japan over the centuries. For the woof, he borrowed grace and refinement from the noblemen and samurai. From the poets' ideal of poverty and loneliness, he chose his warp. To add color and design he went to the artisans: bowls and jars, baskets, bamboo dippers and iron kettles. Finally he pilfered the discipline and depth of Mind taught by the Zen masters, giving his Tea tapestry the strength to endure centuries of wars, revolutions and opulence. It is this very strength which touches us even today, here in America. Rikyu's Tea became a Way for us to move in meditation, surrounded by purity, simplicity and aesthetic refinement.

The world of Tea is a tool for slowing down life, placing each step, each gesture into its proper perspective. But it does not stand of its own accord. Tea is merely a form waiting to be filled by persons in tune with themselves, with the universe.

Tea is both flowing and rigid, the perfect balance of yin and yang, hot and cold, light and dark. It is as masculine as the rustic and rugged tea bowls, as feminine as the touch of silk on graceful fingers. The host is yang, active, giving. The guest is yin, passive, receiving.

When a guest enters the tea hut, his tensions melt into the soft shadows on paper doors. The smell of subtle incense greets him, and one flower in the alcove, stark and beautiful. The sound of water boiling in the iron kettle is like the message of wind through the pines. The guest waits for the mysteries to unfold. But these are mysteries which are not mysterious, like the full moon in a clear sky or a sunrise on a mountain peak. The host enters and bows . . . host and guest, guest and host. The distinctions are clear, the host humbly offers, the guest respectfully receives. Still, with this bow, the two become one, joining energies.

The art takes over completely. With unrestrained motion and concentration, the host purifies the utensils, wiping the tea caddy and tea scoop, washing the tea bowl and whisk. The powdered green tea is prepared, whisked and drunk, sip by sip, one bowl at a time. The utensils are once more cleansed and returned to their original places.

Tea is direct action. Nothing is wasted. Each gesture has been conceived for practical application, style and beauty. Each movement reveals the human form: arms moving in dance-like rhythm, torso straight but yielding like a bamboo forest tossed about in the wind. It is neither the host nor the guest who moves, talks, breathes, drinks the tea. Who is it? "Boil the water, make the tea and drink it!" These are the simple instructions left to us by Sen-no-Rikyu.

It is only after years of Tea practice that its application to daily living can be fully appreciated. What is more satisfying, more complete, more mysterious than lifting a spoon, dipping it into a cup of coffee, watching the ripples evolve and disappear, as we stir, round and round until all the sugar dissolves? Or walking down the street alone, hearing noises and children crying, feeling calm in this solitude. First the right foot, then the left foot, being aware of the body shifting weight, head and back, arms and feet, all in perfect accord, strolling along on the way to the supermarket. Tea room or kitchen . . . where's the difference? Just stirring, just walking, just drinking a bowl of tea.

In the world of Tea we are concerned with the oneness of things in everyday living. A famous Chinese Zen master answered all discursive questions with this response, "Have a bowl of tea!" In offering his tea, he is offering his Mind and body. If you can accept, with your Mind and body, how delicious it will be!

Ecology of Mind: The Sacred

Gregory Bateson

In the last few days, people have asked me, "What do you mean, ecology of mind?" Approximately what I mean is the various kinds of stuff that goes on in one's head and in one's behavior and in dealing with other people, and walking up and down mountains, and getting sick, and getting well. All that stuff interlocks, and in fact, constitutes a network which, in the local language, is called *mandala*. I'm more comfortable with the word "ecology", but they're very closely overlapping ideas. At the root, it is the notion that ideas are interdependent, interacting, that ideas live and die. The ideas that die do so because they don't fit with the others. You've got the sort of complicated, living, struggling, cooperating tangle like what you'll find on any mountainside with the trees, various plants and animals that live there — in fact, an ecology. Within that ecology, there are all sorts of main themes that one can dissect out and think about separately. There is always, of course, violence to the whole system if you think about the parts separately; but we're going to do that if we want to think at all, because it's too difficult to think about everything at once. So I thought I would try to unravel for you some of the ecology, something of the position and nature of the *sacred* in the ecological system.

It's very difficult, as you probably know, to talk about those living systems that are healthy and doing well; it's much easier to talk about living matters when they are sick, when they're disturbed, when things are going wrong. Pathology is a relatively easy thing to discuss, health is very difficult. This, of course, is one of the reasons why there is such a thing as the sacred, and why the sacred is difficult to talk about, because the sacred is peculiarly related to the healthy. One does not like to disturb the sacred, for in general, to talk about something changes it, and perhaps will turn it into a pathology. So rather than talking about the healthy ecology of the sacred, let me try to get over to you what I am talking about with a couple of examples where the ecology seems to have gone off the tracks.

In the fifteenth century in Europe, many Catholics and Protestants were burning each other at the stake, or were willing to be burned at the stake rather than compromise about questions of the nature of the bread and the wine used in the mass. The traditional position, which at the time was the Roman Catholic, was that the bread is the body of Christ and the wine is the blood. What does that mean? The Protestants said, we know what that means — the bread *stands* for the body, and the wine *stands* for the blood. The proposition for which they were burning each other was, on one hand, "the bread *is* the body," and on the other, "the bread *stands for* the body." I do not want to suggest to you that one of these sides is perhaps better than the other, but I do intend that this whole argument is one of fundamental importance when related to the whole of the nature of the sacred and to human nature.

The point is this — that in the various layerings of your mind, or at least in the computer part of your mind (the part in your head), there are various layers of operation. There is ordinary "prose" consciousness — present indicative-type consciousness. That is what you perceive to be true in the sense that you perceive it, i.e., the cat *is* on the mat if you see the cat on the mat. That's the sort of normal waking state that most of us have. In that normal waking state, you are quite able to say that this thing that you perceive can also be a symbol — for example, a stop sign does not actually stop an automobile, but it is a symbol or message that tells people to stop the automobile. You can draw all sorts of distinctions in that normal everyday "prose" space in your mind.

On the other hand, in that part of your mind that dreams, you cannot draw these distinctions. The dream comes to you with no label which says that it's a symbol, a metaphor, a parable. It is an experience that you really have as you dream it; and except in those funny marginal half-asleep states, it's not even something labeled as a dream. That sort of a label is not something which that part of the mind can deal with, or accept.

So now if we go back to the proposition about the bread and wine, we find that to the left hemisphere of the brain, it is perfectly sensible to say that the bread "stands for" the body or is a symbol for the body. To the right hemisphere, the side that dreams, this means nothing at all. To the right hemisphere, the bread *is* the body, or it's irrelevant. In the right side of the brain, there are no "as if's," metaphors are not labelled "metaphors." They're not turned into similes. This is a good part of the problem with schizophrenic people with whom I dealt for a long time. They are more Catholic than the Catholics, so to speak. They feel rather strongly that the metaphoric is the absolute. All right, so there was a religious war — a struggle — between these two sides in the fifteenth century, about the interrelationship of ideas.

Now, it is my suspicion that the richest use of the word "sacred" is that use which will say that what matters is the *combination* of the two, getting the two together. And that any fracturing of the two is, shall we say, anti-sacred. In which case, the Roman Catholics and the Protestants of the fifteenth century were equally anti-sacred in their battles. The bread both *is* and *stands for* the body.

Now, one of the very curious things about the sacred is that it usually does not make sense to the left hemisphere, prose type of thinking. This then can be disastrously exploited in two different ways. It's a double exploitation problem. Because it doesn't make any prose sense, the material of dream and poetry has to be more or less secret from the prose part of the mind. It's this secrecy, this obscuration, that the Protestant thinks is wrong, and a psychoanalyst, I suppose, wouldn't approve of it either. But that secrecy, you see, is a protecting of parts of the whole process or mechanism, to see that the parts don't neutralize each other. But because there is this partial screen between the two parts — the prose and the poetical or dream — because there is this barrier, it is possible to use one side to play with people's emotions, to influence them — for political purposes, for commercial purposes, and so on.

What are you going to do about the *use* of the sacred? There is a very strong tendency in occidental cultures, and increasingly, in oriental cultures, to misuse the sacred. You see, you've got something nice, central to your civilization, which bonds together all sorts of values connected with love, hate, pain, joy, and the rest, a fantastic bridging synthesis, a way to make life make a certain sort of sense. And the next thing is that people use that sacred bridge in order to sell things. Now at the simplest level this is funny, but at another level, it begins to be a very serious sort of business. We can be influenced, it seems, by any confident trickster, who by his appeals makes cheap that which should not be made cheap.

And there's this other strange business with the sacred, and that is that it's always a coin with two sides. The original Latin word "sacer," from which we get our word, means both "so holy and pure" as to be sacred, and "so unholy and impure" as to be sacred. It's as if there's a scale — on the extreme pure end we have sacredness, then it swings down in the middle to the secular, the normal, the everyday, and then at the other end we again find the word "sacer" applied to the most impure, the most horrible. So you get a notion of *magical power* implied at either end of the scale, while the middle is prose, the normal, the uninteresting, and the secular. Now there is the question of what happens in social processes, in human relations, in internal psychology, in getting it all together in one's mind. What happens when the pure end is violated by sacrilege? Of course at once you get various sorts of disaster, so that the pure end confers not only blessing, but also when it is violated, becomes a curse. As all the Polynesian cultures know very well — every promise carries a curse on its tail. So in a sense the double endedness of the sacred is logically expectable.

There's a whole lot which is not understood about this whole species of damage that goes with attack on the sacred. And still less is known about how to repair such damage. This is roughly what we were working on back in the 50's and 60's with schizophrenia — the notion of the relation between the right side, the more abstract, more unconscious parts of the mind, and the left side, the more prose parts of the mind. We found that the *relation* was the vulnerable spot. And that the relation, when damaged, required insight into the nature of the damage on the part of the therapist. So if the therapist is trying to take a patient, give him exercises, play various propagandas on him, try to make him come over to our world for the wrong reasons, to manipulate him — then there arises a problem, a temptation to confuse the idea of manipulation with the idea of a cure. Now, I can't tell you the right answers — in fact, I'm not sure I would if I could, because you see, to tell you the real answers, to know the real answers, is always to switch them over to that left brain, to the manipulative side. And once they're switched over, no matter how right they were poetically and aesthetically, they go dead, and become manipulative techniques.

This is, I think, really what all these disciplines of meditation are about. They're about the problem of how to get there without getting there by the manipulative path, because the manipulative path can never get there. So, in a way one can never know quite what one is doing.

Now this is a very Taoist sort of statement that I've been giving you all the way through. That is, while it may be fairly easy to recognize moments at which everything goes wrong, it is a great deal more difficult to recognize the magic of the moments that come right; and to contrive those moments is always more or less impossible. You can contrive a situation in which the moment *might* happen, or rig the situation so that it *cannot* happen. You can see to it that the telephone won't interrupt, or that human relations *won't* prosper — but to *make* human relations prosper is exceedingly difficult.

There are typological questions here, both in Jungian typology, and in Buddhist typology. There are people for whom a Taoist view of the world is more congenial, others for whom an action-oriented view of the world is more congenial. And perhaps the action-oriented people can do a little more towards contriving what is to happen to others. I don't know. I always find that if I try to contrive it, it always goes wrong.

There are things, you know, that give people like me the shivers. Some people will put potted plants on the radiator — and this is just bad biology. And I guess that, in the end, bad biology is bad Buddhism, bad Zen, and an assault on the sacred. What we are trying to do is to defend the sacred from being put on the radiator, misused in this sort of way. I think this can be done without violence. For example, I remember as a small boy of eight or nine in England, the first

occasion I had to tie a bow tie. For some reason I couldn't get any help, and so I tied a bow, and it stood up vertically. I don't know how many of you have ever tried to *tie* a bow tie. I tried again, and it stood up on end. I then did a piece of thinking which I still think of as one of the great intellectual feats of my life. I decided to put this little twist in it in the first bow, so it would not stand up vertical, but would stand up horizontal — and I did it, and it did! I've never quite been able to think it through since, but I can still produce the little monstrosity when I have to wear one! Now, what have I learned? I learned how to tie a bow tie, yes, but I also learned that it is possible to think through such problems as how to tie a tie, make a pretzel, and other such things. Also, I learned that, having discovered how to do it, I can now do it without all the rigamarole in my head — I've got a trick for doing it. But spiritually, aesthetically, it will never be the same again as that first time, when my whole mind and soul was in the business of thinking how to do it. There was a moment of integration when I achieved it.

All these different sorts of learning, these multiple mandalas, are what we are talking about. It's a matter of how to keep those different levels, rings, whatever, *not* separate, because they can never be separate, and *not* confused, because if they get confused, then you begin to take the metaphoric as absolute, as the schizophrenic does. For example, say I'm learning something less solitary than how to tie a bow tie, say I'm learning to act as a host or a guest, in an interpersonal relationship. Now, the host-guest relationship is more or less sacred all over the world. And, of course, one of the reasons why, to go back to where we started, is that bread and wine *are* sacred objects. Now bread and wine are sacred, not because they represent the body and blood of Christ, but because they are the staff of life, the staff of hospitality, so we *secondarily* relate them with Christ, with sacrifice, and the rest of it. The sacredness is real, whatever the mythology. The mythology is only the poetical way of asserting the sacredness, and a very good way, maybe, but bread is sacred, whether or not you accept the Christian myth. And so is wine. These levels, these modes of learning, and their going along together, are the keys to certain sorts of mental health, and joy.

And before I close, I should say a word about being a scientist. You see, I've been talking to you, not as a priest, or a member of the congregation, but as an anthropologist. And we anthropologists have our values rather differently constructed from those of non-scientists. If you're seriously dedicated to anything, be it art, science, or whatever, that which you are dedicated to is going to be a pretty big component in what is sacred to you. But we scientists are, or should be, pretty humble about what we know. We don't think we really know any of the answers. And this has some very curious effects. On the whole, most people feel that a great deal is known, and what is not immediately knowable they throw into the supernatural, into guess-work, or into folklore. But the scientist won't allow himself to do that. We really believe that someday we shall know what these things are all about, and that they *can* be known. This is our sacred. We are all sort of Don Quixote characters who are willing to believe that it is worthwhile to go out and tilt at the windmills of the nature of beauty, and the nature of the sacred, and all the rest of it. We are arrogant about what we might know tomorrow, but humble because we know so little *today*.

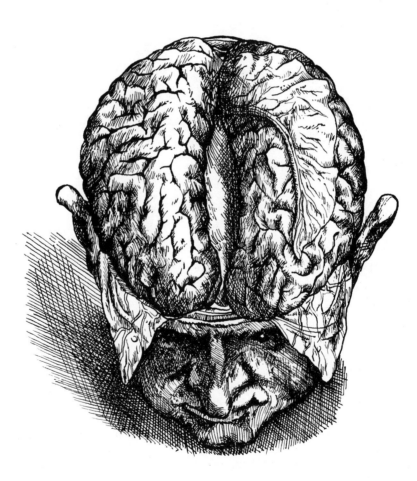

Drawing after the woodcut by Andreas Vesalius in *De Humani Corporis Fabrica*.

A Conversation with Gregory Bateson

Photo by Ellen Pearlman

Gregory Bateson has lived in more realms than most of us allow ourselves to imagine. In addition to anthropology (including the trance dances of Bali), he has investigated schizo- phrenia (the double-bind theory), cybernetics and William Blake. He was one of the first to grasp the importance of ecological thinking.

The particular realm he was inhabiting during this conversation was a house in the mountains just outside Boulder, looking out on hills covered with pine. Walking up the dirt road we picked up a bone (the scapula mentioned below), which we used as a microphone stand.

The interview began before we realized it, and

we found ourselves discussing the arms race as a continuing way of life:

Bateson: Yes, the world repeats itself, such as it is.

Loka: The world repeats itself, could we relate that to samsara, *not only as a circle, but also as a vicious circle?*

So far as the world which I see and live in is concerned, I take it as *samsara*. Obviously every creature, or every species of creature, has to be able to multiply itself with positive gain. If it didn't it would go out at the first epidemic. The epidemic would simply reduce it, it wouldn't come back again. Now, that doesn't mean that

LOKA
28

on that hillside in the next fifty years the pine trees will have done so much positive gain that they will be solid on the hillside. There will be just about the same number on the hillside, believe me, other things being equal.

When does positive gain take effect?

It takes effect when you start kicking the thing down. If I remove 10 per cent of those pine trees, and give them twenty, thirty years to recover, the population will come back to its level. There are all sorts of troubles that arise because the population, to hold that level, requires woodpeckers. That brown pine tree across the way there, he's got the local pine beetle. If they don't get him out, there'll be another half dozen to ten trees with the pine beetle in them in a couple of years. It's infectious. Vicious circles are what biology lives on, but you've got to have a world in which that is all the time being held in control. The springs of the whole system is the presence of vicious circles.

In terms of . . .

In terms of reproduction first of all, Malthusian vicious circles. The more children you produce, the more children they have. That's a vicious circle.

Because sooner or later the population gets beyond what can be supported.

Theoretically the population, if left to itself, will become infinite. In very few generations it becomes larger than the total volume of the earth.

But there is the moon now.

The moon is not habitable for pine trees.

I wonder how that works with the notion of samsara? In earlier Buddhist writings, they literally talk about escaping from birth and death. In the later writings there is the paradox, "Well, yes, it's escaping from birth and death, and no it's not. We're not going anywhere off this vicious circle, we're staying in it."

This is another sense of the phrase "vicious circle." This is the wheel in the *samsaric* sense. This is quite a different thing. By a vicious circle in my sense, I simply mean a tangle of interlocking variables in which the more of something, the more of something else; and the more of the other thing, the more of the first. As opposed to a system which tapers, where it can taper to a steady state equilibrium.

What has never been clear to me about the steady state idea is that it only seems to exist where there is no consciousness in the sense of human consciousness. Where there is human consciousness that element seems to be anti-steady state, because it is always tinkering.

I'm afraid you're right. In that case I would consider it as the Buddhist wheel and say, "I want off!"

I think that is the sense that we may have been talking about. What then is a way out of the circle? We began talking about the arms race.

Which is a particular case. We ran a conference on this point, with my daughter, which is published under the title, *Our Own Metaphor.* The full title was *We Are Our Own Metaphor.* The original title was *On the Role of Conscious Purpose in Human Adaptation.* And the primary memorandum which I sent around to the conference members before we met asserted that the role of conscious purpose is almost entirely antithetical to human adaptation. For just the sort of reason that you were feeling your way towards, that if people would only be good Taoists and leave the cybernetic systems alone, they would run clean and settle to steady state.

After some trauma.

After how much trauma, who knows? The human beings of course can't stand the idea of the intervening trauma.

You could apply that to the idea of the ecology being in a seeming mess right now but in a thousand years, with or without human beings, it might not be in a mess, we could just let it run out.

And we may all be dead, if you call this all a mess.

But would that matter to the eco-system?

No, it could be dead, too. The horrible thing about the god Eco, the gods of the eco-systems, is that they have no free will, no sentimentality, they can be insane (which most gods are supposed to be incapable of). In St. Paul's phrase, they "are not mocked." So if you stand against the eco-system, it's no good saying you didn't mean it, or you're sorry.

Which is the state many of us seem to be at now, saying we made a mistake, but we didn't mean it.

That's about as far as we've got towards ecological insight.

Is it too late?

Ask Eco — he knows, he knows!

To go back to that idea of Taoism — what you're suggesting is that conscious purpose . . .

That Taoism is the abrogation of conscious purpose, yes? This is a part of it. You're not going to worry about whether or not you have cream in your coffee, or indeed whether you have coffee at all. There is a paradox in the whole Taoist thing: are you prepared to say that of the

present 3½ billion population of the world, you are willing to let all go except three million?

That's what you think the earth can support?

I don't know what the actual figure can be, but a lot lower than it is now. You see that we can't let other people do this, let alone do it ourselves. We can't bear it that the Indonesians should have an epidemic. The Dutch, you see, doubled the population of Indonesia simply by introducing vaccination and ordinary quarantine rules.

And you don't think that in the long run that was humanitarian?

I'm sure that in the long run it was not humanitarian. In the short run of course it is, and that's the gimmick. If my little Nora comes down with a disease, I shall get medicine. Even though I don't much believe even in short run medicine.

On the level of your situation you want to use certain things, but on the larger scale which you are aware of, you see that it's a dead end. Penicillin in the Third World has done a lot to make the Third World unliveable.

Penicillin and DDT, between them they have enormously increased the population.

And the paradox is living with these two thoughts simultaneously. It seems that once you have one, there is no way of getting rid of it.

There's no earthly way to get rid of it. DDT they are beginning to get rid of. For one thing, most of the insects have become immune to DDT. Their immunity develops faster than ours.

At the same time that the earth can't support the 3½ billion people, do you think there is something underlying it, some evolutionary growth or movement? Do you see us crashing for sure, or do you see some threshold to be reached, something new to happen?

Well, conceivably always, but what does crashing mean?

Crashing and jumping the threshold might mean the same thing.

Well obviously there are billions who are going to die, just like you and me. Therefore the problem is going to be solved within fifty years anyway. So the problem is going to shift from those 3½ billion to their offspring. We know they're going to die.

You don't think Buckminster Fuller's idea that the problem is just one of mismanagement and lack of distribution and lack of intelligent use of the available energy makes sense?

I don't really believe that, no. Because I don't think the problem is primarily an energy problem. I think it is much more a minor con-
stituents problem. All the other things you need in your food besides calories, practically every element in the table: vitamins, phosphorus, mineral components, so on. These are much more awkward than energy.

And that has to do with complexity.

Has very much to do with complexity, has to do with things being in a scattered state in the world. What we do is to comb the surface and concentrate them. Then having concentrated them, we put them in places where we will never be able to get them back again.

In that light, can you relate Buckminster Fuller to the notion of purpose?

I can relate Buckminster Fuller very easily to the notion of purpose. Have you ever worked on geodesic domes?

Yes, they leak.

They leak, that's right. Why do they leak? Because they are much too purposive. Because they've got no tolerance. The only purpose of a dome is to be a dome.

The people who build them think their purpose is good residence.

I know all that, but Bucky doesn't have any idea what living in something is like.

After all, he lives in airplanes, he says.

That's probably right. But those bloody domes are a very good paradigm for the whole of engineering adaptation.

You might be interested to know that one of the fellows who developed the dome idea at first and who published a number of books, gave it up completely, and went through a long drawn-out ethnological survey of living quarters all over the world, and has decided that the whole approach was much too schematic.

Much too schematic. Straw is much better material to make houses with. Straw and mud make quite good houses.

I'd like to get back to the idea that consciousness itself seems to be a problem, as you're presenting it.

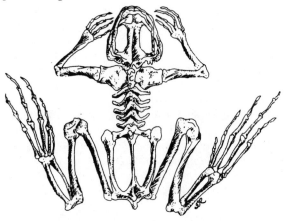

The problem is this: we will imagine a steady state process going along on that hillside of Ponderosa pines, and the pines are balancing out with the deer and the cactuses and all the rest of the living things there. What are they called? "Sentient beings." Now in come you and I, and of the various variables on that hillside, we decide to maximize one. We want more deer scapulas that we can pick up off the surface. Well, obviously, we do that.

To make jewelry with.

Yes, to make jewelry with, it's as nonsensical as that! The first thing is to kill as many deer as you can so the scapulas get around. Well, when we're a little more sophisticated than that, we say, "Well it won't really last, the deer are not so numerous anymore, so if we kill them, we'd better not kill them all." Well, what do deer live on? Deer live on the prickly pear or something. So that leads us to multiply the prickly pear. And if you multiply the prickly pear you disturb everything else. You multiplied it probably by feeding it some special food, or one of those chemical messengers. And then the rest of the balance goes, and so on. Now what happened? What happened was that the human beings identified *a* variable, looked at the immediate predecessors of that variable in the general train, and started with what sophistication they could to maximize these in order to maximize the one they wanted. But they have totally ignored three quarters of the whole circle, you see. All the other things that go together. They go around thinking that the way to explain things is either like that ➤ ➤ ➤ a series of causal arrows, or it branches in ➤ ➤ ➤ ➤ or it branches out ➤ ➤ ➤. You make trains of those things and that is called scientific explanation, understanding. And obviously, if you want more of something here, you make more of what goes into it. But, the fact is that, really, the world looks at least like that ⟲, with then, of course, other branches, and other kinds of feed-ins, from other places ⟲. And if you do what you first thought of, you are going to wreck the balances. And that is all you're going to do, sure as new apples. And that's what that book is all about, *Our Own Metaphor.*

One of the points you made in the Sunday night talk is that we've come to this sort of im- *passe in psychotherapy, changing a man's "I" to suit a therapist.*

This is the schizophrenic's diagnosis of what was wrong with the therapy people were giving him. "A contrivance to change the color of a man's eye to please a psychologist is too much. And you're all psychologists, though some of you turn and become medical doctors, for that part of you which hurts. Never thinking of the man who is so sick he has to munch on his own." That's a hell of a statement.

How do you proceed in psychotherapy then?

Did I tell you his first words when he gave up talking poetry, and started talking prose? They were, "Bateson, you want me to come and live in your world. I lived in it from 1920 to 1943, and I don't like it." He was born in 1920, hospitalized in '43, this was '57. So when Frieda Fromm Reichmann came through Palo Alto, I asked her what she would have said, and she replied, "Yes, I once had a patient who said something like that, and I said, 'But I never promised you a rose garden.' "

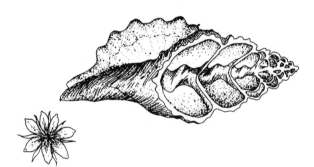

Is this steady state ecology you talk about a rose garden?

Oh no, of course not. It still has epidemics in it very often.

So what are we trying to get out of? Who is trying to get out of it?

You see, lots of people don't see this as a problem at all. Then some Oriental people see those people in the Occident who've got all these dangerous inventions as a result of their monstrous philosophy. So they say, "We better have the same monstrous philosophy." Which is precisely this thing. And this is the differentiated ego, too. Same diagram.

How is that?

We really have a total circuit involving me and the environment, but now we cut that and say, "It's me *versus* the environment." And that cut is a fictitious cut. It cuts across the trains of causation.

How is it that we have the insight to get away from that?

Do we?

Offhand, you proposed Taoism, whatever that might be.

Well, what I really said was that I don't know anybody who could really work Taoism.

It is interesting that when the early form of Buddhism came to China, it melded with Taoism, but there were differences. The early Buddhism in China was called Mahayana Taoism. So there were the Taoists and the Mahayana Taoists at that point. The problem with Taoism, as we conceive it, seems to be that it has absolutely no method, no upaya. Because that is considered to be interfering in a sense.

That's right. Totally un-American.

Very much like Krishnamurti's approach. Perhaps Buddhism seems to take, if not philosophically at least methodologically, a more formal approach, in that instructions are given on how to meditate, which is a paradoxical kind of thing.

'A contrivance to please,' not a psychologist but a Buddhist, 'to change the color of a man's eye.'

The three ways out that I've experienced in my life so far have been, one, political action and analysis; two, psychedelic action and analysis; and three, most recently, meditation and studying Buddhism or the Dharma. Do any of these seem like they will lead to a workable situation?

I have more faith in the second or third than I do in the first. Political action is always more or less self-negating.

Why should that be? What do you think of what is going on in China, for example?

I don't know what is going on in China, but

what little I've seen of their arts and drama, which is all that really comes out that I've had a chance to see, fills me with absolute horror and terror.

Because of . . . ?

The image that comes to mind is of a subcutaneous syringe injecting virtue in large quantities, and over-inflating the whole balloon with propagandistic crap of one kind or another. Now I've not been to China; for all I know they may select the over-inflated items for export.

The arms race seems to be an inevitable outcome of this.

Yes, "Mutual fear breeds peace."

Going back to the ways we have of dealing with this muddle, this vicious circle we're in, we talked about politics and the other two, psychedelics and . . .

. . . and controlled adventures in meditation the third, yes? Well you know psychedelics are very much related to the journey. And I think if you went with Stanislav Grof, you would find that the journey was right there. You would be doing much the same as in meditation. Now what does this do? Suppose that a civilization were predominantly controlled by, and composed of, people who had taken parts of the journey. Individual greed, certainly, would be enormously reduced. You could do this with psychedelics or with ordered Buddhism, ordered, controlled meditation, even mass controlled meditation of various kinds.

But that begins to sound rather . . . how about Chaotic Buddhism?

Ah, but it ain't chaotic, you see. When you begin to talk about a civilization based upon it, then you have meditation halls containing several hundred people. And don't forget that Zen was the backbone of the Japanese army. That can be just as destructive and vicious, and perhaps more so, than at the individual level. But all right, suppose you can avoid that. It all comes back to the arts, you know. Consider the Balinese. They see their land with quite different eyes from ours. They are enormously urban, for one thing. A mass of people close to lots of people, lots of people, all the time. No sense of privacy, withdrawal, no sense of the wild uncivilized nature. If they go for two minutes into the little bit of forest they have left, they squeal like suburban children. "Centipede!" You know, that sort of thing. Now I don't know how that goes in, say, Tibet. It has masses of wild country, whereas Bali has eaten up most of its wild country.

But the question I wanted to ask is, will any of

these things allow us to be part of a steady state system? Rather than being what we seem to be, a sort of virus which destroys its host?

Very much like a virus. The virus destroys the host by self-multiplication. And missionary endeavor. When you kill the host, the viruses are scattered. Ready to infect another. But you persuade the host to make the same sort of proteins as you are. This is missionary endeavor.

Possibly the whole space program is a virus preparing to . . .

Very much so, very metastatic. What was the question about that? Can we somehow not be metastatic?

Can we be an organism that lives in harmony with all sentient beings, realizing that non-organic substances are necessary for sentient beings equally? Or is it still your premise that consciousness itself is the destructive agent?

No. Consciousness becomes the destructive agent by virtue of the other side of the coin. By the fact that it renders unconscious a very large number of considerations. Makes them unavailable, not only unconscious, but rules them out altogether.

Why does it do that?

Attending to x means not attending to y. Attention is perhaps a better word than consciousness. Unconsciousness is inattention.

Then we are trying to say that attention in itself is the problem, in that it must select one thing to pay attention to, to pay attention.

Now we come again to our old friends the EEG's, the yogis and the Zens. As I understand it, the yogis increase their "in"-attention, which is to say they increase their concentration; the opposite side of the thing is non-attention to those things you don't concentrate on. Whereas the Zens learn to avoid concentration, to avoid inner tension by a sort of universal attention.

More than the EEG thing, it seems to dovetail with what Suzuki Roshi and Trungpa are teaching as coming from some common meditation tradition, where there has to be a certain amount of concentration, but you are not trying to get yourself into a particular state by concentration, just choiceless awareness.

Suppose we argue this way: in 1974 we have a certain amount of knowledge of cybernetic subjects, steady states, ecology, but damn little knowledge of the interchanges happening on that hillside. But in principle we have some idea what it is all about, in an abstract way. Now we say, "You eco-cyberneticians, will you please recommend for the world what should be done?" Suppose they say, "We think the cybernetic things are very important, but there is also the aesthetic determinations of what is happening on that hillside." This is a set of regularities in the world of which we have no knowledge. Enough only to say, rather hesitantly, that from the smell of things, it may be so. Now would they be wise to make any recommendations to the world on what to do, when they know there are orders of causation, orders of regularity, about which there is no knowledge? Biological detail, biological principle, patterns. With our little knowledge of cybernetic systems, they can say, "For Christ's sake, don't throw the steering wheel over the side of the car." But as to which road to take when steering, that is something different altogether.

What's your reaction to the Taoist statement that it only takes respect for the intelligence that

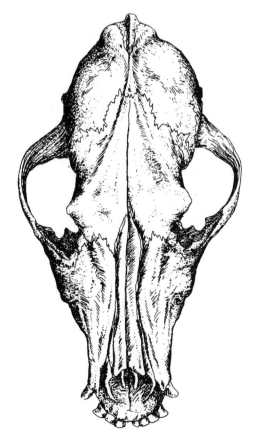

enables the grass seed to grow grass, for the cherry tree to grow cherries?

You obviously can't afford to look at the universe and forget that there are such things as *kinds*. There is a very strong tendency in America to believe that the universe is not made up of discontinuous, separate kinds.

This seems to be a spiritual semi-truth which can turn into almost cosmic soup.

But a pine tree is a pine tree, and an oak is an oak, damn it.

Obviously we began as a part of a steady state system ecology, before we gathered the cybernetic know-how to begin thinking we were controlling it. I wonder if that hunger for sameness is behind our hunger to control things. What is it that leads us to . . .

There is another thing that I think is very important about the human species: that less than a million years ago, man was the low one on the totem pole. He was not an ecological dominant. He was an ecological freak. We were an endangered species. Now we still behave as if we were an endangered species.

It's almost like the youngest child in the family always having that psychological sense . . .

Going around with a chip on his shoulder for the rest of his life. Now this is another whole set of problems: How do you alter the pathway, of say, the house of Atreus? The house of Atreus is the Greek tragedy with the family in which the brother screws the other brother's wife, who then replies by getting the children of that family and cooking them and serving them. All the way down the line to Orestes. We commit these gross things, the Treaty of Versailles, for example. This was a swindle *about* war, not itself a part of war. If you're going to swindle at the peace table you're in trouble. You can do what you like in war, use all the tricks, but you can't get the other side to surrender, and then put your heel on them. That's cheating, and that's what we did. And we (and they) are going to suffer for that for two hundred years, certainly. The whole international crash is part of that. So we've set one of these trains of distrust, feuding and vengeance going, and we have no idea what the mechanisms are for stopping it. How do you eat up bad karma? And if our Buddhist friends have any real idea how to burn up bad karma on an international level, I'm anxious for it, any day.

The metaphor might be to define a space in which the thing can work its way out, as opposed to being in the middle of where it is being worked out. You set a context, an arena where it can happen.

It would be lovely if you can.

Meditation is the context on the personal level.

I agree.

I don't think the Olympics is the context on the international level.

You may build up a tiny bit, but it usually reverses, and the Olympics blows up in a scandal. Someone cheats on the high jump.

Or a team is kidnapped. And that seems to be the situation we are in, where one part of the eco-system is warring on the other part. In Buddhism the human realm is considered the best place to become Buddha, to become enlightened. Maybe it is inevitable that consciousness has developed in human beings as opposed to other species, save perhaps dolphins or who knows what, to a much greater extent . . .

I wouldn't agree with you, but people say that. I think that's a purely racial attitude towards the other animals, in saying they're unconscious. This justifies us in killing them, eating them, frying them.

Yet you're not a vegetarian.

No, but I don't require that justification.

It seems that human beings are the only ones that consciously create this thing which we call art. Am I being human-centric?

The other species are not going to write art criticism for you. So when you say "consciously," that's one of the things you mean, of course.

No, making a painting, or . . .

Oh, well, that's another thing. What about the actual designs of anatomy? I mean why are centipedes beautiful? Whether or not they are beautiful to each other is a question, whether they are somehow internally beautiful, which would not necessarily imply consciousness. To infer that embryology is some sort of harmony, a tune . . .

But whose embryology isn't?

But *I* say, whose isn't? You wanted to confine these things to ratiocinating humans. Most ratiocinations are mainly ugly anyway.

You begin to paint a bleak picture.

I? They're all right, these people . . . God, they are fools.

The conversation continued throughout a lunch that was shared with a family of yellow-jackets. Bateson watched with keen interest as they began nibbling at his chicken and he began speculating on their diet and nesting instincts . .

— Rick Fields
— Richard Greene

Women in the Dharma

Nancy Reimer

Countless are women's defects; my elephantine mind has fallen into the poisonous swamp of guile, so I must renounce the world.

— Naropa

Woman is always a troublemaker.

— Milarepa

Sexual polarity is one of the most binding and oppressive of dualities. Yet within this great tension and dread is tremendous energy for cutting through these forms. The sages Naropa and Milarepa did not escape the sting of woman's discontent, and sometimes sound like misogynists, but they came to understand that "in the Bodhi-Mind, there is neither man nor woman." (Milarepa) Once we know that we are all just human beings, born with male or female organs, and stop being fascinated by the possibility that we are permanently maimed or incomplete, we can get serious.

However it is played, men and women need to understand the double-bind expectations of salvation they bring to one another. Once, upon encountering an old woman who was unaccountably nasty and tried to throw ashes at him, Milarepa said:

Grandmother, you are an angry woman
   and dislike the Dharma! . . .
Grandmother, you are the unpaid maid
   . . . you are burned up with fury.

And he goes on to describe her situation in blinding detail, sparing her nothing:

Grandmother, you are now a wretch,
   half woman and half bitch . . .
Question your thought and your mind
   examine.
You need a qualified and dependable
   Guru.
You should practice Buddha's teaching
And then things may be different for you.

When he had finished, the old woman began to cry, for never had anyone spoken to her with so much directness and compassion. His words were the key to her jail, the jail of ego and samsara. Yet some would argue scornfully that he only offered her the chance to worship at his feet instead of at the feet of her ungrateful male relatives. I must admit that this cynical interpretation was the first to occur to me, since I have experienced my share of anger and suspicion towards men and their solutions for women.

But I went further. What was he really suggesting? Not that she redeem her sunken value through an adoring association with him or by renouncing her own sense and experience. He did not try to lull or seduce her, but only to awaken her. His words, though harsh, contained the germ of reassurance the woman needed.

We do not know if Milarepa became her guru. To my ears, his words to the old lady carry a note of regret, as if to say, "You deserve a good guru. I wish I had time to stay and do this right." How familiar this attitude is to women, along with our corresponding polar attitude of "Stay, love me, and pull me out of the morass I'm in." Of course, the situation is often reversed, with the man playing the pathetic role. So often, tender-hearted and loving, we do stay and try to save each other. Great is our confusion when these well-meaning attempts fail! Yet they are bound to fail as long as we keep trying to swoon our way back to the womb by way of false projections and reinforcing polarity, by refusing to notice the worlds we are actually living in — the man and woman worlds, the inner and outer worlds. We cannot get by just on "love." We need to notice the ropes and swings of escapism we have always used and come down to earth finally. Wonderful fruits really do grow on earth, but because of our distractions and frenzy to project, we have barely tasted them.

We can use Buddhist lore to better understand the "woman problem" by considering the story of Naropa's vision. At the time, he was divorced, a noted scholar, and head of a famous university in India. In his vision he saw an ugly old hag who asked him what he was investigating. He answered that he was studying books on grammar, epistemology, spiritual precepts,

Photo by Ellen Pearlman

and logic. "Do you understand them?" she asked him. He said, "Yes." "Do you understand the words or the sense?" she asked him next. "The words," he replied, at which the woman began laughing and waving her stick in the air. Thinking to gratify her still more, Naropa added, "I also understand the sense." Immediately she began to weep and tremble, and threw her stick down. Puzzled and worried, Naropa asked her what was the matter.

"I felt happy because you, a great scholar, did not lie, and frankly admitted you only understood the words. But I felt sad when you told a lie by stating that you understood the sense when you do not."

This vision had a profound effect on Naropa and was the beginning of his search for enlightenment. He quit his job. He was quite lost and on the verge of suicide when he met his guru, Tilopa.

How shall we interpret his vision? At first I felt annoyed that his vision had to take the form of an ugly old hag. We women get tired of being depicted in dreams, comic books, novels, and films as hags, bitches, vixens — and worse, nebishes. But when I understood that the old woman represented Naropa's own thwarted feminine side, my annoyance drained away and I saw the lesson. I felt humbler. It's all so simple and obvious when antipathy vanishes. Like the repressed anima in Jungian psychology, woman has always represented for man the unacknowledged, miserable part of himself. According to Guenther, the woman in the vision was old because symbolically the female stands for the emotional, which is older than the rational, which in turn couldn't exist unsupported by feelings which it usually misunderstands. She is ugly because what she stands for has not been allowed to come alive in a full, human way. She is a deity because "all that is not incorporated in the conscious make-up of the individual and appears other than and more than himself is traditionally spoken of as the divine." The old, ugly, and divine woman came as a messenger from Naropa's own repressed female side. The force of the message is devastating until Tilopa reveals to him how the source of so much conflict and bondage can become the source of contentment and freedom.

It is no wonder that the Women's Movement has produced so much anxiety in men. There is a double whammy effect: men fear and dislike not only women who won't stay in their place (or are frankly hostile), but the feminine aspect of themselves which, when thwarted, threatens to break out and disgrace them. Women have a corresponding fear of men and of their own undeveloped masculine side. A woman's vision, corresponding to Naropa's vision of the hag, might be of a swaggering, obscenely muscular male with a mind like a computer.

We can be done with the dreamy attitude that an experience with a mesmerizing archetypal member of the opposite sex will bring us through apocalyptic revelations and change our lives. We ought to be glad this isn't the case. Our fears and illusions are addictive, melodramatic, and egocentric; they paralyze.

The "high" that comes from women's recently legitimized anger can be just as misleading. We may blow off a lot of steam, and we may be justified in a sense, but if we look at the results with clarity and precision, we see that we are perpetuating a karmic chain and denying the need for cooperation. As Milarepa reminds us, "Anger is the cause of falling to the realms below." There are many different ways of being aggressive, some of them quite subtle. The motive of revenge is often unconscious, but still present. We are not going to improve matters by becoming bullies, or by treating men as a class instead of individuals. That is what we hated in their treatment of us. These measures do not develop our neglected masculine side, but consolidate our slavishness.

We can choose to proceed angrily, throwing the weight of our moral authority around like swaggering *nouveau arrivistes* (and machos), or we can use our long overdue mandate to work for change with skill and compassion. For this we need our practice of meditation, for by meditating we can see through situations and improve our chances of acting non-defensively and non-aggressively. Our natural dignity does not want us to freak out, sneak, or behave like vindictive underdogs having their day. If we are objective, we will see that men have been as trapped in their roles as women have been in theirs — in some ways more. It is evident that the need of the real world today is not for old-fashioned revenge and aggression, but for the kind of clear, precise, compassionate and democratic attitudes that we foster in ourselves when we cultivate our practice.

The Hundred Thousand Songs of Milarepa, Trans. by Garma C. C. Chang, Harper Colophon (New York, 1970).
The Life and Teaching of Naropa, Trans. and commentary by Herbert Guenther, Oxford University Press (London, 1963).

Toward a Meeting Point of Physics and Buddhism

Jeremy Hayward

In speaking of the totality of what is, Buddhist philosophers of the Yogacara schools and the Tantric practitioners following them refer to the three kaya principles — dharmakaya, sambhogakaya and nirmanakaya. These are three aspects of Buddhahood, the awakened process of being in the world.

In the western tradition no single philosophy has dealt with this totality, as a totality, from the time of Descartes to the twentieth century. Physics has dealt with the object of experience, and religion or psychology with the subject, and this split between subject and object — mind and matter — has been a fundamental thesis of all acceptable philosophies. Furthermore the absoluteness of this split has had a profound influence on the basic attitudes of ordinary people who are neither philosophers nor scientists. It has pervaded our entire world view.

However, in recent decades in physics, and especially in quantum mechanics, the boundary between observer and observed has become quite fuzzy. This has caused much dismay among some physicists who regard "objectivity" as the ideal — in this case objectivity means the irrelevance of the presence of the observer to the results of his observation.

Let us remove this barrier and regard the process of conceiving an experiment, setting it up and collecting data, as the experience of a real human observer — one with feeling, imagination and aesthetic appreciation as well as a discursive mind and a mechanical body, one who acknowledges that his being is inseparable from the world in which the experiment is happening. Analogies between this experience and the three kaya principles now stand out clearly and present the possibility of alternative interpretations of some concepts in physics.

To include the state of being of the observer in our analysis of the nature of an experiment does not mean that we do away altogether with objectivity and revert to the opposite extreme of complete subjectivism. We still recognize that the validity of an experiment depends on the reproducibility of the results by a number of observers. But who are these observers? They must be trained of course. And traditionally they are trained over a period of eight to ten years in a special type of discursive thought, namely physics. But it would seem that the observers most likely to see the real nature of the world are those who are able to take the widest possible view of the totality, rather than those who take a deliberately narrow view and exclude entirely from consideration whatever they arbitrarily decide is irrelevant, including their own state of being. To take this wider view requires a different kind of training, a training in how to live rather than merely how to think. It is often argued that to ignore the state of mind of the experimenter and concentrate on the object is a good and necessary first approximation. The following analogies between physics and the three kayas indicate that this is not so, that in fact the state of mind of the observer is crucially involved at every stage of the experiment.

Dharmakaya. The opening statement: *What.*

What is a completely open dimension. *What* contains no particular actuality, therefore it contains all possibilities. It is timeless space-time, containing flashes of energy. Energy depends on space-time, space-time depends on energy. There is no form, no concept, no proposition. According to Professor H. V. Guenther, "Dharmakaya refers to the presence of Buddhahood as a possibility of actual being." This is the *field* in modern physics. The gravitational field is the space-time manifold which is co-dependent with energy. The quantum field is the set of *potentia* (Heisenberg's word) giving all possible results of all possible experiments. The search for the one unified field is the search for dharmakaya. Thus the field is neither purely "physical" nor purely "mental," but is apprehended by the noetic mind as the mental pole of the totality.

Sambhogakaya. First movement: *How, where, when?*

Contains tendencies to move. Particular possibilities are aesthetically valued. Definite questions which contain limited possibilities as answers are imaginatively felt. This is the level of communication and of cosmic law. "Sambhogakaya is empathetic Buddhahood. It brings into prominence the factors of imagination and feeling" — Guenther. This is the experimental arrangement, including the body-mind of the experimenter, whereby he asks what form energy has, how it flows. It is the directional quality of energy when we cut the four-dimensional manifold, by a particular perspective, into three dimensions of space and one of time. Order and natural laws are appreciated at this level. It is in the experiment that the mental pole communicates with the physical pole. The particular perspective determines what laws will be "found."

Nirmanakaya. Final statement: *This or that.*

Particular possibilities become actualities. Form arises, the completed manifestation. Instantaneous events, point-instants, are actualities. Apparent endurance, as things, is the repetition of pattern from event to event. Apparent motion is due to slight changes in this pattern. "Nirmanakaya is embodied Buddhahood. An individual becomes the concrete realization of Buddhahood." — Guenther. This is the totality of a moment of experience which, only in abstraction, can be analysed into sense-percepts, color, sound, etc. A click in a Geiger counter, a flash in a spark chamber, a feeling of certainty, the moment of recognition of the pattern on a photograph. All these are the data of physics.

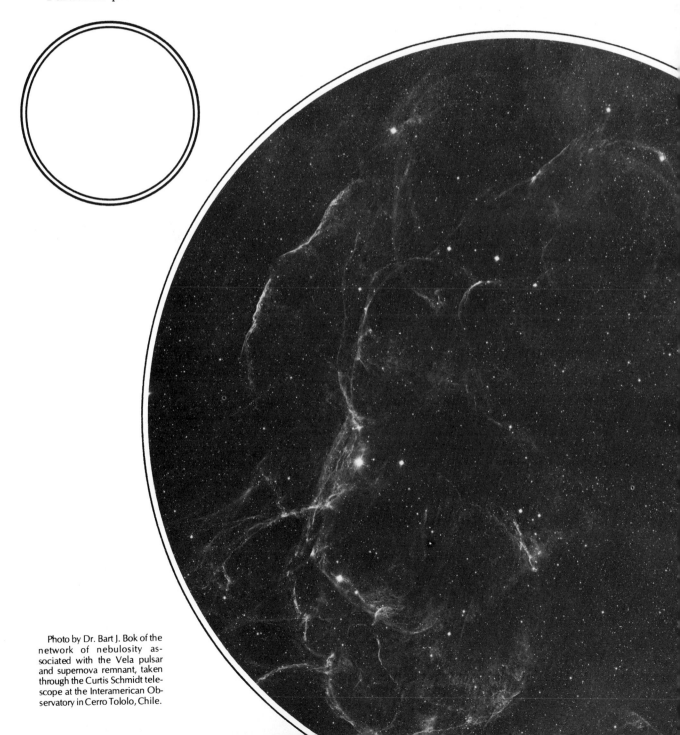

Photo by Dr. Bart J. Bok of the network of nebulosity associated with the Vela pulsar and supernova remnant, taken through the Curtis Schmidt telescope at the Interamerican Observatory in Cerro Tololo, Chile.

Theatre and Space Awareness

The Fabulous Invalid: now more than ever, her sickness and sores so obvious that even "theatre people" can no longer ignore the stench rising from the stages of the world. Alexander Cohen agreeing to meet with Richard Schechner. What could that possibly mean? Perhaps they are still looking for new medicines to cure theatre, artistic antibiotics, better and bigger bandages. More high rise cultural centers. Physical plants where janitors get paid more than artists. Underground parking. Who is working for whom here?

Why are they working?

Why are *they* working?

And the invalid just lies there and bleeds. It's an old story.

Last winter I talked with the director of one of the largest regional theatres in the country about creating a laboratory or research workshop for the acting company. The purpose was to introduce new techniques and exercises into the company to keep them abreast of the times. This is something all good businesses do with their executives, scientists, etc. In other words, a conservative yet vital function which is done to insure growth and development in the parent organ so that it does not turn inward on itself and devour its own self for food. This famous director sincerely explained that there is no room for this kind of experimentation in the current theatre. This made sense, since in her own words the only stipulation of the two million dollar Ford Foundation grant was "to build the finest theatre in the world, which we did." And her proud smile stayed on her face three or four beats beyond believability, and the situation became very clear and grotesque. Two acres of deep pile carpet. Video-monitored parking. All to produce *Life with Father*, or Edward Albee as an *experiment*.

What made the situation all the more painful was the knowledge that during this whole operation there is no anesthesia. The director said, "I know we need it, the experimental

Photo by Ira Mazer

John Morrow

program. We're cutting off our own heads without it."

So cut them off. And please hurry. This neomorte* is still bleeding and won't give the world the courtesy of departing gracefully. Rather like an old actor still taking his curtain calls long after the audience has gone home to watch tv.

I suppose theatre started bleeding severely around 1725 or (insert your own date). An almost fatal coma set in around 1800. Then around 1890 a hiccup was detected in Russia, and the corpse got up off the table and almost walked out of the morgue. Planetary situations (including World War I) took their course and back to the death bed for theatre with a few coma-like memories of that walk fading into and out of reality now and then. Thank you Mr. Artaud.

So if that is the background of our theatre

---

*Neomorte — a biologically functioning cadaver, minus the nervous system — legally dead.

and the hope of the present theatre, why bother? Forget theatre. It's forgotten. Now what?

Why is theatre at Naropa? What is theatre at Naropa? Macbeth with mindfulness? Buddhist propaganda under the disguise of far-out space awareness techniques, so we can go back to our old reactionary selves, and really enjoy them this time with the new costumes? No. I don't think so, if we watch it closely. There may be something unique in theatre, and it may be happening here at Naropa.

The conditions are fertile to give birth to a new concept in theatre that has been forming for the past several years or so in lofts in New York City, centuries ago in Indian villages in Mexico, in Gypsy camps in Portugal, and wherever serious theatre is practiced.

Right now the most distinguishing characteristic that is developing in this theatre is *space awareness*. And in a community where the concept of space awareness is supposedly a daily practiced habit, it is only natural that Naropa would provide a compatible and nurturing home. A new theatre opening up all sorts of new concepts — just what is theatre, what is art? And it is this that gives me the faith now to keep doing what I envision theatre to be, and to do it here.

Coupled with this newness is the old-fashioned continuity of this just being the next logical step of theatre history. A continuation of Shakespeare and Stanislavski, with a large dose of Einstein. Coupling one's vision of a milky white light of enlightenment with the acceptance and possibly real experiencing of those Black Holes. And all this coming in a theatrical framework. By that I mean, rather than going to an interesting corner in Boulder and zapping my mind into "space awareness," and then sitting back to enjoy the show, I find I am still doing workshops, still forming groups, still doing productions, whether over an entire city or in a 25 x 25 room.

It seems that theatre has for the present time fairly well investigated, to the point of boredom, the mental, social, and psychological aspects of art. By developing the theatre, or art, through a physical investigation of the environment, i.e., feel, touch, smell, sight, sound, we have culminated in a sensory overload or Garden of Eden of neurosis, that is if we truly did that trip thoroughly. Of course a lot of theatre just pretended to do it, but *Dionysius 69* probably did it. Groups like LaMama's Plexus group were doing it also.

The emotional environment was very ably explained away by the Actor's Studio and those that followed in its path. And currently Growtowski is keeping us informed on the actual instrument of perception itself — the actor's body. The physical plane leading to the other planes.

All of these methods and processes had to be strained through the intellectual representation of someone's vision (the playwright) to produce the actual play. Often the playwright was not connected to these processes, at other times he was intimately involved from the beginning. It didn't seem to matter much either way as this part, the writing or content, was usually the weakest link, due to small vision.

Ensemble work is the main ingredient. It must be as good as the Open Theatre was, or the Living Theatre was, or the Iowa Lab theatre, or the 1971 N.Y. Knicks championship team was.

So space awareness theatre is growing out of the best of all the above, and focusing on space, wherever it may appear. And it appears in the emotions. The environment. The senses. The body. The mind. And it appears in the weirdest ways if one keeps watching it. It appears between the words when talking to another person. The meaning of the words seems to be formed more in the space before the word and after the word than within the word itself. So the actor gives the space at least equal meaning and consideration as the matter (the word).

The space between the actors. The emotional and psychologically colored space. The non-colored space. How does that change things? The space before movement begins — before movement fills space — after movement has left it.

Knowledge and familiarity with these aspects of space in relation to theatre then determine the actor's action for him. The actor is receptive to the space, lets it happen within him as he passes through, lets us see it clearly, and then goes on. The actor is then, once again, a transparent vessel of the Dharma, rather than putting onto the space his ideas, emotions and neurosis. It is a spontaneous discovery, happening in front of and with an audience, a discovery which encompasses them both.

In this context, instead of the actor taking the psychological and physical and social make-up of his character to define himself, all of which is limited by the mind and its perceptions, he takes space as the starting, or focal point, and by doing this, *discovers* the situation that is already happening, rather than *making* the situation or action. This brings to the surface the reality of the moment, and makes it the dominant reality, the reality that seems to be underneath the surface of our lives, shaping and controlling them. This forces the actors to deal with the real situation happening between themselves. And by dealing with that moment the actor then makes and forms his actions. His emotional and physical reactions can only be in truthful response to the situation that is currently happening right now. If he is a good actor, he deals with it creatively; if he is not an artist, he deals with it therapeutically.

This method disallows theatre to have the unreal luxury of a preconceived notion of what will happen on stage that night. The actors will have to deal with and respond creatively to whatever reality the actor finds there, directly and truthfully. Good training for life. 'A long walk on a short pier' sort of thing. And it is all much more vital and theatrical than: "Oh, I am going to be angry here (at 9:15 thursday night) . . . so you be sure and do this . . . so I can get to be angry." In which case things start getting very predictable, and set, like a lot of our lives already are, and getting removed from the reality of the moment, and audiences start nodding out on corners all over the country, and it is coma time again.

This process or kind of theatre is not for everyone, and most theatre people balk at it with the words, "It's not theatre." But I have found in the past that people who are interested in this kind of theatre, and those who have a talent for it, are generally very well trained actors, with all kinds of theatrical experience from Broadway to Balinese dancing, or else total amateurs who do not have a preconceived notion of what theatre "should be" . . . like dope ad-

dicts, the mentally retarded, psychotics, and true artists wherever they are. As familiarity with this process develops into finer technique, we can then create with the space, sculpt the reality of the moment, and bring theatre back to art. All we have to do is just "see" it, and create with it.

"And it is on the Space where there is nothing, that the utility of the wheel depends."

That knowledge of Lao Tze's gives us a fine starting point. An Aleph. And for our particular Drama we know our Wheel isn't quite as classical as Lao Tze's, but more like the broken hoop in Black Elk's words:

"The nation's hoop is broken and scattered — there is no center any longer and the sacred tree is dead."

Now what?

yours in the void
John Morrow

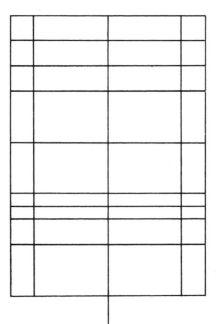

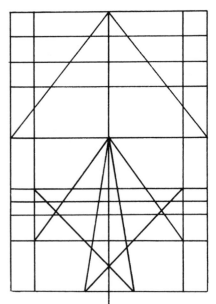

How to Draw the Buddha

L. Gyatso

From the moment you are inspired to draw a Buddha, be aware of your mind state. One should try to eliminate all aggressive frustrations and impatience by pinpointing their nature and source, replacing such emotions by being gentle, kind in thought, and elegant in movement. This elegance of movement, speech, and thought is brought about by deep breathing and eliminating tension. The mental approach of drawing Buddha is threefold: primarily one is drawing the historical Buddha Sakyamuni, but also the enlightened essence of one's teacher, and also that of oneself. Therefore, the three aspects of Buddha should be remembered: boundless compassion, transcendental wisdom, and power over illusory mental projections, and thus also over illusory reality itself.

Patiently and with much analytical

perception, one should study the grid line drawing for Buddha, making mental notes of the relevance of each line and the points along it which indicate particular points on Buddha's figure. This preliminary study and understanding of the relationship between the grid lines and the figure is of the utmost importance, for thereafter the actual practice of drawing becomes automatically premeditated. Furthermore, as one would not think of walking upon, disrespecting, or carrying under one's sweaty armpits one's guru or the symbol of one's own primordial mind, in the same way one should treat Buddha images and even the drawing apparatus with due respect and mindfulness. One's attitude is the basis for, and thus more important than, the external action.

The serenity and harmony of Bud-

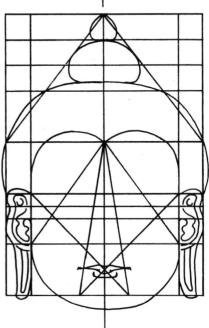

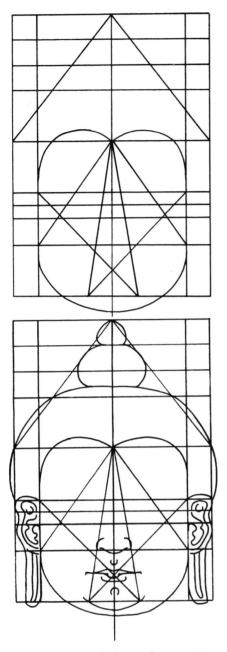

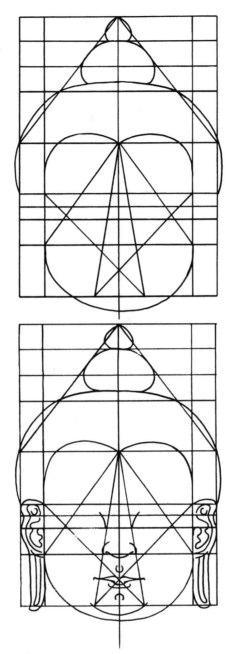

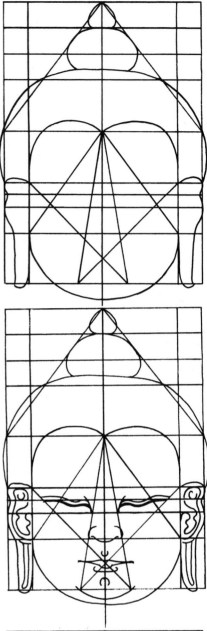

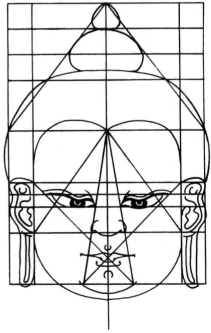

dha's image and physical proportions are an expression of great beauty and represent the physical manifestation of Buddha's enlightened mind. Every detail of his image is meaningful, even the small spot between his eyebrows marking the eye of wisdom. According to ancient Indian conceptions and aesthetics, the Buddha's figure is that of the highest physical form of a spiritual being (Sanskrit *Mahapurusa*) and therefore is not based on mundane standards of beauty. Buddha Sakyamuni is generally depicted in the Nirmanakaya form, wearing monk robes, lacking ornaments, seated in the *vajrasana* yoga posture. His right hand is in the *bhumi sparsa* mudra symbolizing the calling of the earth to witness his enlightened realization and victory over the "seductive sense world." His left hand rests in the

dhyana meditative mudra, holding a begging bowl symbolic of his simple ascetic existence.

The size of the units used to measure out the grid is variable according to the size of the image one wishes to draw, but retaining the proper proportions is essential. Having first drawn the base horizontal line and the vertical central line, measure out the grid rectangle. Use a calibrated straight edge from which you can calculate appropriate units—e.g., for a 8½ x 11 inch size paper, ½ inch will be suitable as representing four units. Then, having ruled out all of the horizontal and vertical grid lines, carefully join the appropriate intersection points to derive the grid diagonals. Once the grid lines have been drawn accurately, commence by drawing the chin and jaw lines, then the forehead and hairline, and then outer head and hair lines. Notice that there is a protrusion at the top of Buddha's head (Sanskrit, *shaha-srara cakra*) which is the enlightenment center, from whence appears the *ushnisa*, the flame top which rises from the head of a fully enlightened being. Then draw in the outline of the ears, taking note of the long earlobes, another mark of an enlightened being. It is very important next to draw the armpit to the waist and hip lines before drawing the neck and shoulders in. The relevance of this order becomes apparent especially when drawing a figure whose upper portion is slightly leaning to either side (e.g., Manjusri, Tara, etc.). All the time being aware of the total body, whether the

lines have been drawn yet or not, continue to draw the hip to knee line, and then the legs and feet. Notice that the soles of the feet are visible due to his *vajrasana* position. Then draw in the arms, elbows, wrists and hands. Finally draw the details of the ears and face, leaving the eyeballs until last.

The lines should be drawn with such precision and feeling of identification with the figure being drawn, that a minimum of two hours seems necessary for the drawing of the Buddha without clothes. It is also a very good idea to continue to draw the grid line and the lines of the head in order to perfect the facial details, for it is the face, hands and feet which convey most the beauty of the Buddha's im-

age. This is a daily practice on which one might spend from six months to a year as an artist's apprentice in Tibet. Therefore the apparent simplicity of this drawing should be given a second thought, and many repetitions with consistent, if not growing, mindfulness seem fruitful. The important fundamental attitude is to be projecting the Buddha image and essence from within oneself, and not to be merely copying a form which one assumes to be an external reality.

To conclude, I hope that boundless freedom will be found continually from these strict, rigid and age-old lines.

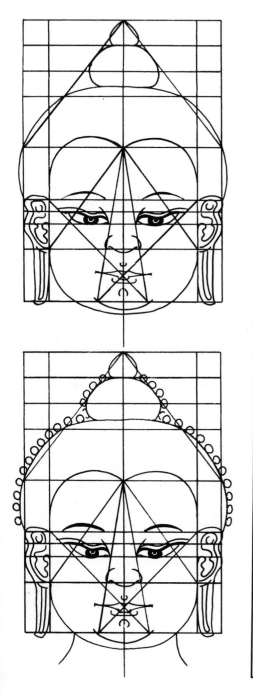

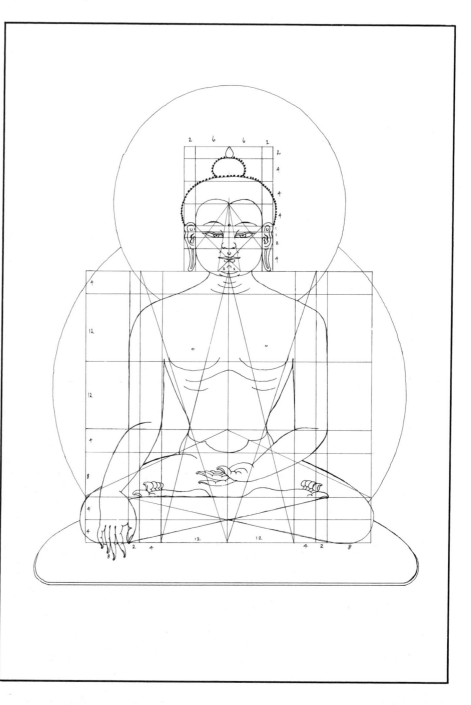

Communicable Diseases

Fictions by Joshua Zim

Photographs by Susan Ross

She had been hunting without rest for nearly three days and nights, but none of her most intricate and cunning traps had been successful. She knew she could not afford to fail, and there was little time left. For some hours now she had been refusing to acknowledge the desperateness of her situation, as if it were some clumsy brute which she could still subtly sidestep, but clearly there could no longer be any hope of success. For all her skill, she had discovered not a single trace of her prey, not a track of any kind. She had explored impossible terrain with grim persistence, and not a single contact had been made. There was no way to turn back; she could think of no way to move on. She made a small fire and sat with her back to it, gradually falling into a state of paralysis.

Hours passed and her body grew rigid. The sun rose indifferently, and she was no longer conscious of light and dark. In the plausible emptiness between the molecules of her being, she was a frozen element in suspension.

More hours passed.

Arising from nowhere and sweeping over the earth, the stink of excrement and sweat and rotting flesh filled the air around her. It burned her nostrils and throat, her eyes, and she became dimly aware of an ashen beast slowly approaching her, its presence borne on a hot, choking wind. She screamed, breaking her paralysis, but she could not escape. It covered her completely . . .

By nightfall it was finished with her, and in some manner she could not apprehend, it suddenly contracted itself to an ordinary scale. Unexpectedly, it assumed a posture of submission before her. She nodded in silent agreement, and built a cage for it, then returned to civilization.

For some years she traveled around the world with the diminished beast on display, and all who came to see it were overwhelmed with dread. They were deeply, unconsciously grateful that she had somehow been able to capture it. She became famous.

The beast vanished from its cage one night in mid-winter. In the morning she was found crouching in fright, unable to speak, or move, or make any sign of recognition whatsoever.

If you will let go of your standpoint, you will perhaps understand that the focus here is neither the beast nor the woman, but the fiction which implicates us all. "When we communicate a feeling to someone, something which we can never know happens at the other end. All that we can receive from him is again an expression. This is closely analogous to saying we can never know when in Fizeau's experiment the ray of light reaches the mirror."

What sign can we make, passing in the darkness? Who is Fizeau?

A bar is a singular and vital place; if it is genuine, it does not disclose its character readily. Like a woman who has lost her obvious charms, a good bar is patient and allows itself to be discovered slowly. A bar is cunning; it permits a man to do nothing, to know that he is doing nothing, and to feel that it is all right that he is doing nothing. He has gone to a bar and he is doing nothing. He is musing, contemplating, talking, arguing, watching, reflecting; doing nothing. He has left his private solitude to share a common solitude, and it is all right; he knows he is doing nothing, and it is all right; he is doing nothing, and it is all right; he is reflecting, watching, arguing, talking, contemplating, musing, and it is all right. He has gone to a bar and he is doing nothing and it is all right. A bar is parochial. It has an inescapable point of view. Like a woman who has lost her obvious charms, a bar may be dangerous. It is, after all, a drinking place.

Bourbon was the drink of the day. How he had made this choice, what darkened recess of the heart had called for this baptismal spirit, he did not know; the decision was irrevocable. The choice of drink is the imagination of a world. He is drinking his fourth drink, there is no manner of human thought he is discriminating against, and he is playing chess badly. Ordering a fifth drink, he appears suddenly preoccupied; he drops the chess game and the bartender is wary. Where once he was doing nothing, he is now doing something, and a subterranean wildness resonates in the bar. The bartender is big and gentle and wary. The wildness is an odor, an outline for things. The wildness is American, it is the breakout for open space, the instinct for the open road.

He is drinking his fifth drink without refuge, and he is swept entirely beyond any resting place. He is stalking himself; the bartender is on edge; there is no mystery in any of this, the choice of drink is the imagination of a world. The wildness has jumped the gap and is in both of them now; they are creatures and their antagonism confuses them and is real.

Drinking

Transmission

Chien Sun Li suffered loss of face. She did not, in fact, say she had suffered loss of face, since to do so would have meant still greater loss of face. She was silent and she made no sign whatsoever that she had suffered loss of face, and yet it was understood that she had suffered loss of face. Of course it was possible she was merely simulating loss of face by remaining silent; her silence suggesting to sympathetic observers, who had packed the courtroom, that she was experiencing loss of face when in fact she was not. Had she spoken about loss of face, however, these observers would have regarded the entire affair as a sham, and in this case Mrs. Li would assuredly have felt much loss of face. She could presumably have declared that she was not suffering loss of face, but by doing so she would have made certain that no one believed her. As it was, Chien Sun Li remained silent and she made no sign whatsoever that she had suffered loss of face and it was understood by all that she had suffered loss of face, and this was felt to be a most serious thing.

When Mrs. Li arrived at San Francisco International Airport on a flight from Hong Kong, she was arrested by U.S. Customs Agents. One of the carved wooden statues she was transporting inexplicably split open. It was the Bodhisattva Kuan-Yin. Four pounds of high grade heroin were discovered in the image. Mrs. Li disclaimed knowledge of the drug.

At her trial, she insisted she had been duped by members of Hong Kong's wealthiest circles; in particular, she mentioned a gentleman named Mr. Ting. Discreet inquiries were made by the Hong Kong police, but absolutely no evidence of the existence of Mr. Ting could be found. Mrs. Li, who required a translator at her trial, declared that he was a patron of Buddhist temples throughout Asia. She declared that he had entrusted her with the ancient religious statues for transport to Buddhist communities in the United States as gifts. She declared that he had offered her $5000 for the task, since the statues were of incalculable value and she was worthy of his trust. She could offer no clue, however, regarding the alleged whereabouts of the vanished Mr. Ting, and she was found guilty as charged.

Because there was no evidence presented to indicate that Mrs. Li was herself a wholesale trafficker in narcotics, she was viewed by the court as merely a carrier for persons unknown. She was fined $5000. She was ordered deported. The judge indicated that this was a just and compassionate sentence, and that the penalty could have been far more severe. Mrs. Li felt loss of face.

She did not say she felt loss of face. She was silent and she made no sign in any way whatever that she had suffered loss of face and yet it was obvious to sympathetic observers in the courtroom, who had come to observe in the courtroom the loss of face of Chien Sun Li, that she was not merely simulating loss of face but had indeed suffered loss of face, much loss of face, and this was felt to be a most serious thing. Imprisoned to await deportation, Mrs. Li hung herself.

After her death, Chien Sun Li found herself in the Jade Palace of the Western Paradise. There Mr. Ting greeted her warmly, and the Jade Emperor himself apologized for any inconvenience that might have been caused her. Mrs. Li bowed politely.

"It is necessary for the Dharma to take root in the West," explained the Jade Emperor. "For this purpose and in these difficult times, we are obliged to employ Mr. Ting. He is an honorable servant of the Dharma, to be sure, but as with all the inhabitants of the human realm, his motives are clearly his own."

I suppose this tale is homage to Kerouac, lonely dharma brother and to spear-eyed Burroughs, and to Kuan-Yin, who delivered the goods . . .

Beer cans

I could not bear the brilliance of the morning or the bitterness in my heart. Slaughter. The harpsichord tones of The Art of the Fugue were no comfort, but sounded the slaughter of the innocents, and the deep moan of the universe. I sat in my window, like the rest, and I watched.

I watched them carrying him out onto the snowy street, into the ambulance, his grey skin stark against the whiteness and everywhere, behind shades lifted slightly from windows the neighbors, Portuguese, Irish, Italian, the working poor of Somerville, watching, silent, Sunday; the bored ambulance drivers hauling his heavy stupored alcoholic body and his face was scarred by a thousand unredeemed failures, his wife accompanying him in stockinged feet, enraged at him and his weakness, enraged at herself and her slavery, enraged at her children and their ingratitude, enraged at her friends and their betrayal, enraged at her neighbors and their curiosity — the seething gnawing anger of her, stumbling with her dignity in the fresh wet snow but before this it was at night her boy came by, he was seventeen, he could find no work he was deadending everywhere and he said he'd signed up with the marines but he needed her o.k. and she screamed she'd never send her kid to get his balls blown off by some stupid stinking chinee bastard and mister president of the U.S. of A. you can take your fucking war and fold it up eight ways and tuck it where the sun don't shine and the family had a fight over it a brawl actually there was nothing else to do, so by morning she'd given in and then later when he went off for training she finished a six-pack and staggered out into the street in the moonlight cursing the motherfuckers who'd stolen her son so they'd stay fat and she cursed everyone who'd ever crossed her in her entire life beginning with his royal fucking majesty Jesus H. Christ who by this time — and could he hear it — had better crap or get off the pot cause for her money she'd take the devil ANY time and moving in decrescendo through all the complaints and troubles of her unremarkable life right down to finish with a coda for Rita Hernandez you spic whore who left the washing machine covered with lint and whose sheets crawled with comestains and God, take care of my boy. Sweet Mother Mary, I don't even know how to ask anymore, just take care of him, don't let him get killed, or shot up, don't let him lose no arms or legs, don't let him get the clap from them slanty cunts, he's just a baby, don't let him turn queer, don't let him get hooked on drugs, don't let him hurt no one, Lord, I don't want him to hurt no one, I raised him not to fight even if some punk kid took something from him I told him it ain't his anyway, the way you said Lord, I don't want him to hurt no one. God! Lord, please we're just nothing, fucking beer cans you kick in the street, Lord please, why'd you give him to me if you're gonna take him away

the next day her husband drank himself to his final sullen death and she did not weep but maintained her dignity cause the neighborhood was watching like a flock of scavenger birds so she did not weep though her heart was scraped raw she rode with his corpse in the ambulance and she did not weep but just endured, which was all she had left to do while the snow blanketed the world in white and mocked its awkward sweating sorrow.

Tribe

Jacob Kohn was an unremarkable, impeccable man. He used Breakstone's Unsalted Butter on his toast, ate Grade AA Extra Large eggs, and drank two cups of Maxwell House coffee, Regular Grind, every morning. His wife was the tragedy of his life. On the back of his right hand, nestled between the V of the two veins that swelled manfully there, a small dark circular wound caught his attention. He had two sons. They were the only remaining statement of his collapsed ambition.

Jacob Kohn smoked Camels. Although he had been in America many years, he still occasionally held his cigarette between thumb and index finger; it was a spacious, European gesture. He had never struck his sons, neither in play nor in anger. He drank his coffee black, sucking it through a rectangular piece of Domino sugar held between his teeth. His younger son wondered how he made the smoke come out his nose.

"Come here, I'll show you a trick." Jacob Kohn's merry eyes delighted the boy.

"So, if you watch very carefully, I'll make the smoke come out my ears. But, you'll have to pay attention, or you won't see it." The boy could not believe this but still it was his father.

"Here, press your hand here against my chest. That's right, like that, to help push the smoke. And watch my ears."

The boy pressed his right hand against his father's chest and stared at his father's ears. Was that smoke coming out?

With a clean, elegant gesture, Jacob Kohn removed the cigarette from his mouth, and lowering it slowly, pressed the glowing tip into the back of the boy's right hand, between the V of the two veins barely visible there.

"Don't trust anybody," Jacob Kohn pronounced flatly.

He was a master of twentieth century indigenous American yoga by the age of ten. The esoteric meaning of Nancy Drew's backing her red roadster over the limp body of a one-legged Arab lying across her driveway was immediately clear to him. By the time he was in high school he could smoke a cigarette, listen to the radio, fondle a breast, sip a beer, calculate the speed and intentions of drivers moving in at least four directions and push his own car to the limits of its machine perfection all at once; careening round the wild curves of the Bronx River Parkway, or pressed tight to the rail of the East Side Drive at speeds, relative to the fixed reference point of his ancestors astonished bones groaning here and there beneath the earth, of 65 to 105 miles per hour. He could cruise. He had no need to pay particular attention to any of his processes. He drove on his breath, and he cruised for speed, he cruised for precision, he cruised for power. And he was serious, because he knew death cruised with him. He could, with a slight turn of the wheel, head into a concrete embankment and snuff out his physical life; if he chose, he could cross the shimmering yellow double line and mangle the lives of other travelers; as an adept, he could maneuver his vehicle so skillfully that it moved beyond the bonds of compulsion into the realm of spontaneous action. At such moments, his own being redacted from certainty to mere plausibility.

He rode the thruways; he rode the freeways; he road the highways of American liberation, his essence in motion, if not motion itself. You could not accurately speak of his existence; it was, like matter, simply a suggestive statistical probability. His cruising sang the high-pitched song of the world's lament and exultation.

Of course, the whole affair is tinged with romanticism. It is Oklahoma at 2 a.m. and a car suddenly jumped the dividing line and came straight at him. He was alone. He swerved to the right, hit the soft shoulder, hit a ditch, rode on two wheels in an exquisite and balanced curve, riding space, riding time he had it made and uncannily aware and then, just as he felt to recover his rear right tire blew and his car smashed into a tree. The other driver, a young female initiate who had just received her license, was pierced through the chest by the steering column of her Chevrolet, and died instantly, in an explosion of pain.

He was thrown from his vehicle and caught on a barb-wire fence thirty yards from the tree. He hung there for three hours until a farmer discovered him and called an ambulance. His skull was fractured, his ribs punctured a lung, his legs were broken in several places, but he survived.

Vehicle

His recovery was miraculous and inexplicable to the doctors treating him. He spoke little, and tested the refinement of his faculties. His senses of touch, smell, hearing, and taste were acute, beyond anything he had experienced before. But his sight bothered him. He could not describe or analyse for the doctors what had changed, but he felt a sickness of the eyes. They concluded it was an hysterical reaction which would work itself out in time, and suggested psychological counseling. He decided to get back in a car and drive.

He checked the rearview mirror. Adjusting the angle, he noticed his view seemed to expand beyond the scene reflected from behind. He had an uncanny sense of the future springing from the image in his mirror. He realized his eyes were fixed to the mirror, and only with extreme concentration could he draw them from it to the front windshield. Before him incomprehensible chaos swarmed, and he grew dizzy. He returned to the rearview mirror, and unhesitatingly accelerated to about 90, watching the past recede from his vision into the future, knowing that now there could be no choice but to keep the vehicle forever moving, until it wore itself out like a banner disintegrating in the wind.

The one-legged Arab yawned.

Communicable disease

Of course, if you stir things up you take a chance the gods will notice you. They're always looking for an opportunity to exhibit their powers; if you ask for something, BAM! Before you know it, they've showered you with heavenly flowers, incense, perfumes, oils, ointments, garments and robes, wreaths, all sorts of divine odds and ends. If you're a nervous type, they may send you into acute bliss; the very least you can expect is a mild euphoria. Love will seek you. Good fortune will begin to haunt you. The universe will become your own overstuffed armchair, confortable and smelling familiar.

There are some drawbacks, however, that ought to be mentioned. Heavenly robes, for instance, are almost inevitably a size too large, and are likely to make you look slightly ridiculous; bliss leads to despair; when love is gone, hatred will find you; good fortune is bad luck. People will forever be wondering who you are; they'll want proof of your mystical powers, they'll insist on knowing your station and which of the forty-nine planes you occupy; they may resort to measuring your brainwaves; those who are jealous may turn to auric attack. You may be unable to find a decent pair of shoes.

Only let the gods discover you, and you will be forced to take to joys and sorrows like birds take to flight; those poor miserable creatures compelled to ride the winds, battering themselves against the flat indestructible air, which is nothing, and means nothing, and intends nothing.

The gods do not notice stones. Stones have no yearning, and so cannot be other than what they are. Let your heart be as a warm stone, glowing in the afternoon like warm eyes on the grass, dissolving with slow precision. Let your heart be as a warm stone, and the gods will let you be. They won't even know you exist.

I didn't think I'd ever be giving you advice. I didn't think I'd have anything to say at all. But I look at things and words come; I suppose I've got some sort of communicable disease.

Herbert V.

Guenther

Tantra and Contemporary Man

There are, even in the Buddhist context, different connotations and different explanations of the term "tantra." In Tibet, the tantric tradition has been kept alive. In India, Buddhism had practically died out, and was only reintroduced in its earlier form, the Hinayana, after the impetus given by some English residents in Ceylon to further the study of the indigenous way of thinking. Later on, greater emphasis was placed on the study of the Sanskrit texts. Then with the influx of the Tibetans, purely philosophical exegeses and the application of these ideas were combined within their own lives.

In the *Guhyasamaja Tantra*, the earliest tradition which we have as far as an Indian work is concerned, "tantra" is defined as "actuality grounded in inalienableness." This is one possible interpretation. The emphasis here is on actuality; it deals with what is immediately present, with what we encounter without resorting to hypotheses or dogmas which distract us from the basic problem of how man is to grow, or from the basic question that underlies the question "What is man?", but not in the sense that the answer has already been given before the question has been asked. Actuality is seen in a much wider context, a spacious context that also deals with the specific human individual, because wherever one goes, one meets individuals. Man meets man and not some abstraction, and he has to deal with this problem.

Here, we have a further division or explication. I use this word "explication" deliberately because even in a philosophical context it is not the task of a philosopher to explain, but to explicate. If he is honest, he starts with what is actual, with what is real, and he tries to fit this into a context which will be meaningful — a context within which he himself can interact with his environment, whether his environment be nature or even other human beings. Man is never alone but is always with others within a world which is as much his making as that of others. So here we have a further explication of the word "tantra" referring to man as a possibility, a starting point. We begin with man, and the question then becomes how is it to end with him? — not as a dead end but as a worthwhile specimen in the whole universe. So this also is tantra, the term here referring to that which we would say *makes* man while he *is* man. This is further explicated as an open dimension illumining, interpreting, shedding light on these existential modes of Being which then shine forth as his actions within the world. The way man goes about doing this constitutes his experience.

Experience, of course, is a tricky word. In this context, it is not so much a question of the content of the experience, but the very possibility for man to experience and to learn. This refers not only to the tantric tradition but also to the whole of Buddhism. The process of life is a continuous and continuing process of learning. This process of learning is a progression; it does not necessarily mean an improvement. Improve-

ment is always a rationalization that we add to the process. A progression and a learning process have many failures or successes. It is on this wide emphasis and wide basis of tantra that we start and then try to narrow it down to the concrete individual.

The concrete individual, which we conceive in the traditional way, and to a certain extent also in the Tibetan tradition, is a compound of mind and body. But as I have pointed out in my book, *The Tantric View of Life*, this division to which we are so much accustomed does not apply because the dualism of body and mind is not native to the tantric tradition. There, body and mind are seen always as a unity. We do not have a body without a mind (if that were the case, we would have a corpse) and neither do we have a

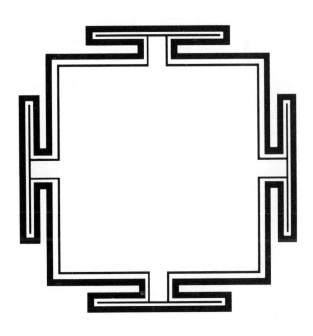

mind without a body. The interrelationship is so tightly knit that it is better to say that what we call the body is not an abstraction or an entity as might be found on the dissecting table or on the operating table in the medical theatre, but is a living entity. In this way, the body is much more properly understood as the embodiment of psychic life.

That the body is an embodiment of psychic life is one of the important features of the tantric tradition, and as such, the body is also a creative force which is active and which is moving and following certain patterns which we set up. What we would call the mind is not what we ordinarily understand as the center of egocentricity about which we, in ordinary life, are so much concerned. Mind is the creative point, the spark, that radiates.

Here we are back to the initial point that the actuality is one of radiation which occurs also on other levels, and so the body is always the bearer of a life force. In so far as the body occurs in this particular situation as lived experience, man is both subject and object. This is one of the most significant contributions that tantric discipline has on the philosophical level. There is never a mere object and there is never a mere subject; subject and object are together. I

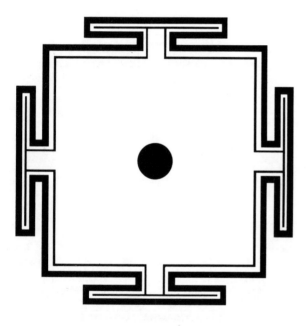

feel myself as subject and I am at the same time present to the other as object, just as the other is subject to himself and cannot help but present himself to me, the observer, or the other person, as object. Each of us wants to be treated as subject; we want to see ourselves not as a mere entity to be manipulated, to be controlled, or to be disposed of.

Here we have the further division which we call an exteriority (the object) and an interiority (the subject). When we want to be recognized as subjects, we automatically introduce the idea of value. Certainly, the body is a value; there are few people who would dispose of it voluntarily. We speak of it as a value concept in so far as there is an intrinsic value of the body which is not arbitrarily assigned. Our body is our way of existing, our way of Being — and by virtue of Being, it is valuable. Being is valuable not because of values assigned to one as a scientist or as being an asset for some business organization. These values are no values because they are arbitrary and have nothing to do with Being. Tantra emphasizes and speaks about the body as a very valuable and precious entity which is not an abstraction, but Being in the division of *dharmakaya*, *sambhogakaya*, and *nirmanakaya*. These ideas of the three *kayas,* so often translated as the three bodies, are not physical entities or abstractions, but are ways in which man experiences a world made up of the subject-object unity.

The *dharmakaya* is the experience of being-as-such. It is an interiority which is also present as an exteriority, because while we are with others, we are also at the same time tied and connected with our own existential state. This kind of empathetic being in which we are drawing our strength from our very existence is technically referred to as the *sambhogakaya.*

In this empathetic being — which we perceive and which we feel, because it is as much a perception as it is a feeling — we have also the apprehended meaning of Being in the symbols of many colors and many hues. In this respect, every one of us is valuable in his own right, is also a *nirmanakaya*, or as the Tibetan texts say, a *tulku.* The *tulku* is not reserved to one individual, but each of us is one in his own way, except that in ordinary life one always overlooks this fact. Thus, we turn to the question of the body or the mind, and in trying to evaluate the one over the other, another question arises. In the tantric tradition, we want to know what really *is*, we want to go to the very bottom, to the very source of our being which we cannot define beforehand without falsifying the whole process. We must make a start, a beginning. But we must also know that this beginning is not a beginning in a historical sense; it is so only in a logical way. We have to start somewhere, but where we start does not imply a beginning. What we observe, what we conceive and how we feel is always in a continuum and therefore excludes an end as a dead end.

All Buddhist texts, whether in the Prajna-paramita literature or in the tantric tradition, speak of a beginning of a path and a goal. Although they create the concept that one arrives at or achieves something, they also make it clear that the goal of Buddhahood is not a static entity, because it is part of the Buddha activity to help and serve, because it is grounded in Being and in knowledge. It is not grounded in a fictitious being such as the ideas we have about what might be the case or the utopia that is so predominant in various philosophical trends and other disciplines.

Being, or in a more narrow sense, the body, is referred to in various ways, one of which is *mahamudra*, the encounter of Being with itself. It is an overarching, and in this sense, a transcending function, because it is not somewhere else. The moment it would be somewhere else, it would lose its value. If we postulate a transcendent, or an absolute that is over and above the phenomenal, or that which is here, we have already relativized it and have lost sight of what is there. This is indicated in various texts we have, whether we follow the bKa'-rgyud-pa tradition which has its foundation in the teaching of Naropa and his spiritual teacher, Tilopa, or whether we follow the rNying-ma-pa or the old tradition. In each case, we start with the immediacy of Being, the immediacy of experience, and the immediacy of observation, which is not based on subject-as-such or on an object-as-such, but which combines these things and knows what is there.

In this cognition there is also a response and in this response to a presence we are at once cognitively responsive and feelingly responsive. The division that we traditionally make between knowledge and feeling does not apply. It is an artificial introduction and because of its artificiality it is a distortion. Feeling and cognition go together; they are only two sides of the same coin.

We want knowledge and lapse into opinion. There is never any absolute truth. Truth is only satisfied curiosity and there is no reason ever to be satisfied. So here the starting point does not preempt the case, nor does it prejudge the nature of man. Actually, in knowledge, we want to know what is the real nature of man, and we are not satisfied with a sham manifestation of it. Therefore, the way of getting into knowledge is

to go into what is technically known as the "way."

The "way" in Buddhism is not an inert link between two stages like a highway linking two cities. The way is the going itself. It is a process, a progression of growth and of growing awareness. But in order to be aware, I must have something before me, and again, we automatically have the split between subject and object; but, this applies only to the way, not to the ground from which the diversion as division into polarities occurs. We must always be aware of the fact that the way is not an inert link between what we call the starting point and the goal, but that it forms a unity. It is the manner in which Being as a dynamic facet and as a totality manifests itself and presents itself, and in so

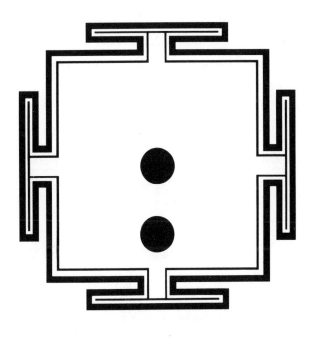

presenting itself, invites judgment.

Here we have two levels of operation. Technically, that with which we start and that with which we deal is known as the *bodhicitta,* which is translated as enlightenment thought or an attitude directed toward enlightenment. The term *citta* is a very wide one and does not tally exactly with what we understand by the term "mind" because in the Buddhist philosophical tradition, it has been more a catalyzer which sets a number of mental operations into motion. In Buddhist philosophy the idea of the mind as a container with which Western philosophy is so concerned is completely absent, and therefore, we should be careful not to read things into a system which are not there. One important division which prevails in Buddhist philosophy is knowledge. Knowledge is not given for itself but given so that we may act. We cannot separate activity from life, but activity is not the same as activism or busybodying. So here we have to be very careful that what we encounter is an open dimension which may be differentiated but which never loses its character of openness. We have openness which is technically referred to as *shunyata,* and its active aspect is known as *karuna,* which is translated as compassion. *Karuna* is compassionate action, but it is not on the level of sentimentality with which we too often

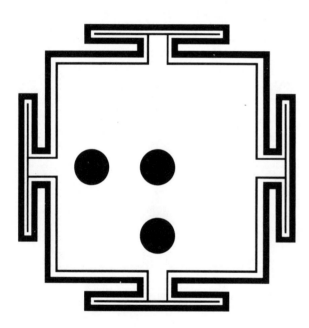

confuse it and which we identify as compassion. Although the word *karuna* is derived from the Indian root *kr* meaning "to act," *karuna* is action based on knowledge

The second level is the cooperation or the interaction between *thabs* (upaya) and *shes-rab* (prajna). *Shes-rab* is a function, a mental event within the structure of which the term "mind" has been given. It is basic and as the term implies, it is a heightened view, a heightened application of the basic capacity that is in man, and it is discriminative. Discrimination has,

very often, a negative connotation, but we can do nothing but discriminate, which means that we single out something and find out more about it. Therefore, it is also an appreciation. So *prajna* is a very complex fact. It is both discriminative and appreciative. It is discriminative in that, in the framework of knowledge, it can distinguish between that which is real and that which is merely fictitious, and in so far as it can do this and can concentrate on that which is real, it can also appreciate. This brings us to another important point: in order to know properly, we must also be appreciative. Opinion denies any appreciation. In *karuna,* we have a dialectical movement in which knowledge — appreciation — must find its enactment in our lives.

Buddhist tantrism always starts with the idea of the situation. This is a very empirical observation. Man is always in a situation which has a character of tension. Wherever we are, we are in a situation and because of the tension, we try to resolve it. In most cases, when we try to resolve tension, we find ourselves in another situation often worse than the one we had before. Thus, it is all the more important to discriminate between that which is real and that which is merely fictitious. To the extent that I learn more about the situation, I can act better and feel much better with an existing situation. In this framework, the situation remains, but it has changed its character. There is interaction in the manner in which I deal with others, and the interaction also reflects my way of seeing another person.

This brings us back to the very beginning — we want to be treated as subjects and not merely as inanimate objects. But now, this means I have to recognize the subject character of the other, and in recognizing this, I automatically recognize his or her value. I then act on the basis of value. The action of value is to preserve, to appreciate, and not to destroy. So we have action that enhances the awareness of the value of Being and of the person. It is here that symbolism comes in so very strongly and this has given rise to the misconception of what tantra is about. When we are in the world, and in the situation, the situation is always made of individuals who are males and females. If we indulge in object thinking, we think of "What can I do to her?" or "What can I do with her?" And in many cases, people who do not go beyond this kind of thinking believe that all of this can be summed up in the notion of sex. As a consequence, they amass such fantastic notions that they display an outcome of their utter ignorance of tantra by giving their books such titles as *Tantra: the Yoga of Sex*.

In tantra, we are in closer contact with what is there. This is referred to in the images of *dakinis* or in the fact that *prajna* is feminine and that enactment is masculine. Here two things come together — the what and the how. *Prajna* is the how, that is, the appreciation "How does it feel to be?"; and the enactment, the *upaya*, says "What is it to be?" We cannot have one without the other. If we try to deal only with the "what" we may have statistics but we leave out very important factors: how this whole situation looks, how we can go about it, how there can be the connection, the tradition of what one has to do in the framework of preserving the value and the whole issue of the reality of Being.

Because appreciation is an integral function of *prajna*, one other key term is *mahasukha*, great bliss, as it is literally translated. The term "great" is used not in the sense that there is something smaller or something larger, but it is used in the sense that something could not be greater than it is. In this technical, linguistic jargon, *maha* here is the elative; it is the optimum level of being fully alive. So here again, tantra deals with a purely empirical basis. When we are at the maximum or optimum level of our feelings we are also most appreciative. But too often we lose it. This loss makes us realize the optimum level of being fully alive and makes us try to find out how to recapture this moment which was considered to be the most worthwhile experience a person could have. So the idea of "great bliss," the *mahasukha*, becomes one of the central ideas. Every deviation from this is felt as a frustration — the lowering of the capacity of the potential that is man. This lowering of the capacity has both a cognitive and feeling component or tone. When we lose this feeling of being at our peak, we see everything gloomily in the light of frustration; thus, the Buddhist idea that life is frustrating. Frustration is a reminder that something has gone wrong. We cannot define frustration (duhkha) simply in negative terms; we must see it as an indication that something has gone wrong and that something has to be done about it.

This is connected with the idea of radiation. A person who is fully alive radiates into his environment. It is not by chance that we say one sees things in a rosy light, or that one can electrify and stimulate others. When we lose this sense of awareness, this state of being at the optimum level, and things turn gloomy, we have the beginning of *avidya*, which is the lack of pristine awareness but which still is cognitive in that we no longer see things as-they-are but see them through the fictions we create about them and take these fictions as the real. *Avidya* is not only cognitive, it is also one of the basic emotions which distort our vision because it means the light has gone out. It is groping in the dark, and due to this groping we make mistakes and fail to realize and to see the value of Being and

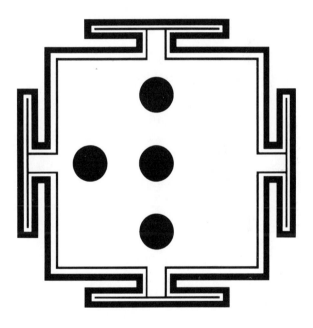

judge existence in the framework of the fictions that we have developed instead of seeing things as-they-are. So the indication that the light has gone out, that we are in a state of frustration, acts as a tremendous stimulus to find out what has happened. We ask of ourselves, "Why did the light go out?" and the moment we ask this question, we already have anticipated the answer.

This frustration can be dissolved, though not abolished. One cannot say, "Oh, I'll go and dump it somewhere." This is impossible. But it can lose its hold. Remember this: problems are never solved, problems dissolve. They lose their hold over us. This is to recapture the way to be fully alive.

So we have again introduced the term "the way" so common to Buddhism. "The way" is an unfolding and a broadening — a widening to such an extent that we can no longer say that there is a periphery, that there is a limit, because the moment we introduce a limit we have already destroyed man and his whole Being by having set up a pure fiction, a pure fancy, into which we try to fit the living individual. This fiction which is knowledge obscured by the emotions becomes a travesty of the pristine awareness that is basic to life. Once the pristine awareness falls, all is lost and from this come the emotions such as cupidity-attachment, infatuation, and so on. We then postulate and create ideas which are purely

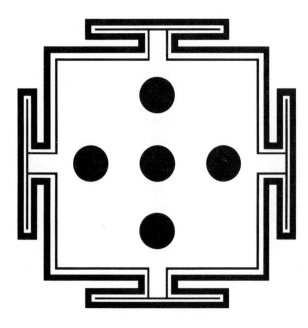

fictitious and dominated by unfulfilling demands.

When we come to the goal we have to be or to develop our situation. We should not have expectations because there is not a single entity in the whole realm of reality that can fulfill expectations or demands which we might make on it. This applies, in particular, to the human situation. Expectations and fear go together. They are obverse sides of one and the same phenomenon, so we have to learn how to see things as-they-are. So far as we talk about things as-they-are, we are again in a situation, but this situation is considerably changed. Here we come to

real Being, not a fictitious being. And we can also communicate. Communication is not talk or the endless noise that goes out over the loudspeaker. Communication can even be effected without words. A gesture can be more communicative than an hour-long talk.

We see in terms of what we call "mind," but this mind is not one which deals with the fiction of an ego or a self (be it the phenomenal self or a transcendental self). We see the mind as action. We can and do act on the basis of knowledge. This knowledge, we might say, is a phenomenon or a function of the mind divested of its egocentricity. We are on the level of that which is referred to as Buddhahood, which means that all the obscurations, all the interpretations and fictions we have put upon ourselves from our very limited perspective, have dissolved. Now the openness, the richness that cannot be subdued or subsumed under a concept, persists. This is how the term *Buddha* was understood by the Tibetans, and also in the Sanskrit, where it means a "waking up." The moment we wake up, the world is revealed to us with nothing excluded. We can see, look at, and appreciate the world. But the moment we get drowsy, the world looks gloomy and we try to justify it, to rationalize it, only to reinforce the frustrations that grow with the fictions and the demands we make from them. This is termed *samsara*.

Samsara is one aspect or one interpretation we give to this continuous task of being and becoming man as a never-ending task, inspired, maintained, and supported by what in words we would call Buddhahood. Each one of us has the capacity to have this peak experience if we exert ourselves. But exerting ourselves does not mean to develop fixations, to strain. The moment there is strain, there is no longer any free movement. This is what we call in tantric technical language the "fetter." But where there is no fettering, there is also no necessity for liberation. Let us have a look before we seize things. And with this look, the path begins. At this moment, when we have divested ourselves of all presuppositions, when we can look at things as-they-are without interfering with them, then we can start and travel the way which will lead to the goal that is not a dead end. This is in short the Tantric View of Life.

The illustrations on pages 55 to 60 show the traditional sequence of development from the unmanifest to the complete five buddha mandala.

The Great Liberation Through Hearing in the Bardo*

A new translation of the "Tibetan Book of the Dead"
by Francesca Fremantle

with an introduction and calligraphy
by Chogyam Trungpa

There seems to be a fundamental problem when we refer to the subject of *The Tibetan Book of the Dead*. The approach of comparing it to the *Egyptian Book of the Dead* in terms of mythology and lore of the dead person seems to miss the point, which is the fundamental principle of birth and death recurring constantly in this life. One could refer to this book as "The Tibetan Book of Birth." The whole thing is not based on death as such, but on a completely different concept of death. It is a "Book of Space." Space contains birth and death, space creates the environment in which we behave, breathe and act; it is the fundamental environment which provides the inspiration for this particular book.

The pre-Buddhist Bon civilization of Tibet had very accurate indications on how to treat what is left behind by the dead person, the footprints so to speak, or temperature, left behind when he is gone. It seems that both the Bon and Egyptian traditions are based on that particular type of experience, a way to relate with the footprints, rather than a way of dealing with the person's consciousness. But the basic principle of *The Great Liberation Through Hearing in the Bardo* is that of the uncertainty of sanity and insanity, or confusion and enlightenment, and the possibility of all sorts of visionary discoveries that happen on the way to sanity or insanity.

"Bardo" means gap; it is not only the interval of suspension after we die, but also suspension in the living situation; death happens in the living situation as well. The bardo experience is part of our basic psychological make-up. There are all kinds of bardo experiences happening to us all the time, experiences of paranoia and uncertainty; it is like not being sure of our ground, not knowing quite what we have asked for or what we are getting into. So this book is not only a message for those who are going to die and those who are already dead, but it is also a message for those who are already born. Birth and death apply to everybody constantly, at this very moment.

— Chogyam Trungpa

*An excerpt from *The Tibetan Book of the Dead: The Liberation Through Hearing in the Bardo* translated from the Tibetan with commentary by Francesca Fremantle and Chogyam Trungpa. To be published in the late spring of 1975 by Shambhala Publications, 2045 Francisco Street, Berkeley, California 94709. © 1975 Francesca Fremantle and Chogyam Trungpa. All rights reserved. No part may be reproduced in any form without permission in writing from the publisher.

The First Six Days
of the
Bardo of Dharmata

The dharmata bardo is the experience of luminosity. Dharmata means the essence of things as they are, the is-ness quality. So the dharmata bardo is basic, open, neutral ground, and the perception of that ground is dharmakaya, the body of truth or law.

— Chogyam Trungpa

Calling the dead person by name, one should say these words very distinctly:

"O son of noble family, listen carefully without distraction. There are six bardo states: the bardo of birth, the bardo of dreams, the bardo of samadhi-meditation, the bardo of the moment before death, the bardo of dharmata and the bardo of becoming. O son of noble family, you will experience three bardo states: the bardo of the moment before death, the bardo of dharmata and the bardo of becoming. Of these three, the luminosity of dharmata in the bardo of the moment before death shone until yesterday, but you did not recognize it, and so you had to wander here. Now you will experience the bardo of dharmata and the bardo of becoming, so recognize what I will show you without distraction.

"O son of noble family, now what is called death has arrived. You are not alone in leaving this world, it happens to everyone, so do not feel desire and yearning for this life. Even if you feel desire and yearning you cannot stay, you can only wander in samsara. Do not desire, do not yearn. Remember the Three Jewels. O son of noble family, whatever terrifying projections appear in the bardo of dharmata, do not forget these words, but go forward remembering their meaning; the essential point is to recognize with them:

Now when the bardo of dharmata dawns upon me,
I will abandon all thoughts of fear and terror,
I will recognize whatever appears as my projection
and know it to be a vision of the bardo;
now that I have reached this crucial point,

I will not fear the peaceful and wrathful ones, my own projections.

"Go forward, saying these words clearly and distinctly, and remembering their meaning. Do not forget them, for the essential point is to recognize with certainty that whatever appears, however terrifying, is your own projection.

"O son of noble family, when your body and mind separate, the dharmata will appear, pure and clear, yet hard to discern, luminous and brilliant, with terrifying brightness, shimmering like a mirage on a plain in spring. Do not be afraid of it, do not be bewildered. This is the natural radiance of your own dharmata, therefore recognize it.

"A great roar of thunder will come from within the light, the natural sound of dharmata, like a thousand thunderclaps simultaneously. This is the natural sound of your own dharmata, so do not be afraid or bewildered. You have what is called a mental body of unconscious tendencies, you have no physical body of flesh and blood, so whatever sounds, colors and rays of light occur, they cannot hurt you and you cannot die. It is enough simply to recognize them as your projections. Know this to be the bardo state.

"O son of noble family, if you do not recognize them in this way as your projections, whatever meditation practice you have done during your life, if you have not met with this teaching, the colored lights will frighten you, the sounds will bewilder you and the rays of light will terrify you. If you do not understand this essential point of the teaching you will not recognize the sounds, lights and rays, and so you will wander in samsara.

"O son of noble family, after being unconscious for four and a half days you will move on, and awakening from your faint you will wonder what has happened to you, so recognize it as the bardo state. At that time, samsara is reversed, and everything you see appears as lights and images.

"The whole of space will shine with a blue light, and Blessed Vairocana will appear before you from the central Realm, All-pervading Circle. His body is white in color, he sits on a lion throne, holding an eight-spoked wheel in his hand and embracing his consort the Queen of Vajra Space. The blue light of the skandha of consciousness in its basic purity, the wisdom of the dharmadhatu, luminous, clear, sharp and brilliant, will come towards you from the heart of Vairocana and his consort and pierce you so that your eyes cannot bear it. At the same time, together with it, the soft white light of the gods will also come towards you and pierce you. At that time, under the influence of bad karma, you will be terrified and escape from the wisdom of the dharmadhatu with its bright blue light, but you will feel an emotion of pleasure towards the soft white light of the gods. At that moment do not be frightened or bewildered by the luminous, brilliant, very sharp and clear blue light of supreme wisdom, for it is the light-ray of the Buddha, which is called the wisdom of the dharmadhatu. Be drawn to it with faith and devotion, and supplicate it, thinking, 'It is the light-ray of Blessed Vairocana's compassion, I take refuge in it.' It is Blessed Vairocana coming to invite you in the dangerous pathway of the bardo; it is the light-ray of Vairocana's compassion.

"Do not take pleasure in the soft white light of the gods, do not be attracted to it or yearn for it. If you are attracted to it you will wander into the realm of the gods and circle among the six kinds of existence. It is an obstacle blocking the path of liberation, so do not look at it, but feel longing for the bright blue light, and repeat this inspiration-prayer after me with intense concentration on Blessed Vairocana:

When through intense ignorance I wander in samsara,
on the luminous light-path of the dharmadhatu wisdom,
may Blessed Vairocana go before me,
his consort the Queen of Vajra Space behind me;
help me to cross the bardo's dangerous pathway
and bring me to the perfect Buddha state."

By saying this inspiration-prayer with deep devotion, he will dissolve into rainbow light in the heart of blessed Vairocana and his consort, and become a Sambhogakaya Buddha in the central Realm, The Densely Arrayed.

But if, even after being shown, he is afraid of the lights and the rays because of his aggression and neurotic veils, and he escapes, and if he is confused even after saying the prayer, then on the second day Vajrasattva's circle of deities will come to invite him, together with his bad karma which leads to hell. So, to show him, one should call the dead person by name and say these words:

"O son of noble family, listen without distraction. On the second day, a white light, the purified element of water, will shine, and at the same time Blessed Vajrasattva-Aksobhya will appear before you from the blue eastern Realm of Complete Joy. His body is blue in color, he holds a five-pointed vajra in his hand and sits on an elephant throne, embracing his consort Buddha-Locana. He is accompanied by the two male Bodhisattvas Ksitigarbha and Maitreya and the two female Bodhisattvas Lasya and Puspa, so that six Buddha forms appear.

"The white light of the skandha of form in its basic purity, the mirror-like wisdom, dazzling white, luminous and clear, will come towards you from the heart of Vajrasattva and his consort and pierce you so that your eyes cannot bear to look at it. At the same time, together with the wisdom light, the soft smoky light of hell-beings will also come towards you and pierce you. At that time, under the influence of aggression, you will be terrified and escape from the brilliant white light, but you will feel an emotion of pleasure towards the soft smoky light of the hell-beings. At that moment do not be afraid of the sharp, brilliant, luminous and clear white light, but recognize it as wisdom. Be drawn to it with faith and longing, and supplicate it, thinking, 'It is the light-ray of Blessed Vajrasattva's compassion, I take refuge in it.' It is Blessed Vajrasattva coming to invite you among the terrors of the bardo; it is the light-ray hook of Vajrasattva's compassion, so feel longing for it.

"Do not take pleasure in the soft smoky light of the hell-beings. That is the inviting path of your neurotic veils, accumulated by violent aggression. If you are attracted to it you will fall down into hell, and sink into the muddy swamp of unbearable suffering from which there is never any escape. It is an obstacle blocking the path of liberation, so do not look at it, but give up aggression. Do not be attracted to it, do not yearn for it. Feel longing for the luminous, brilliant, white light, and say this inspiration-prayer with intense concentration on Blessed Vajrasattva:

> When through intense aggression I wander in samsara,
> on the luminous light-path of the mirror-like wisdom,
> may Blessed Vajrasattva go before me,
> his consort Buddha-Locana behind me;
> help me to cross the bardo's dangerous pathway
> and bring me to the perfect Buddha state."

By saying this inspiration-prayer with deep devotion, he will dissolve into rainbow light in the heart of Blessed Vajrasattva, and become a Sambhogakaya Buddha in the eastern Realm of Complete Joy.

Yet even after being shown in this way,

some people are afraid of the light-ray hook of compassion, because of their pride and neurotic veils, and they escape. So then on the third day Blessed Ratnasambhava's circle of deities will come to invite them, together with the light-path, to the human realm. So to show him again, one should call the dead person by name and say these words:

"O son of noble family, listen without distraction. On the third day, a yellow light, the purified element of earth, will shine, and at the same time Blessed Ratnasambhava will appear before you from the yellow southern Realm, The Glorious. His body is yellow in color, he holds a wish-fulfilling jewel in his hand and sits on a horse throne, embracing his consort Mamaki. He is accompanied by the two male Bodhisattvas Akasagarbha and Samantabhadra and the two female Bodhisattvas Mala and Dhupa, so that six Buddha forms appear out of the space of rainbow light.

"The yellow light of the skandha of feeling in its basic purity, the wisdom of equality, brilliant yellow, adorned with discs of light, luminous and clear, unbearable to the eyes, will come towards you from the heart of Ratnasambhava and his consort and pierce your heart so that your eyes cannot bear to look at it. At the same time, together with the wisdom light, the soft blue light of human beings will also pierce your heart. At that time, under the influence of pride, you will be terrified and escape from the sharp, clear yellow light, but you will feel an emotion of pleasure and attraction towards the soft blue light of human beings. At that moment do not be afraid of the yellow light, luminous and clear, sharp and bright, but recognize it as wisdom. Let your mind rest in it, relaxed, in a state of non-action, and be drawn to it with longing. If you recognize it as the natural radiance of your own mind,

'H*

* Calligraphy for LOKA — the six syllables of dharmata, by Chogyam Trungpa.

LOKA
64

even though you do not feel devotion and do not say the inspiration-prayer, all the forms and lights and rays will merge inseparably with you, and you will attain enlightenment. If you cannot recognize it as the natural radiance of your own mind, supplicate it with devotion, thinking, 'It is the light-ray of Blessed Ratnasambhava's compassion, I take refuge in it.' It is the light-ray hook of Blessed Ratnasambhava's compassion, so feel longing for it.

"Do not take pleasure in the soft blue light of human beings. That is the inviting light-path of unconscious tendencies, accumulated by your intense pride. If you are attracted to it you will fall into the human realm and experience birth, old age, death and suffering, and never escape from the muddy swamp of samsara. It is an obstacle blocking the path of liberation, so do not look at it, but give up pride, give up your unconscious tendencies. Do not be attracted to it, do not yearn for it. Feel longing for the luminous, brilliant yellow light, and say this inspiration-prayer with intense one-pointed concentration on Blessed Ratnasambhava:

> When through intense pride I wander in samsara,
> on the luminous light-path of the wisdom of equality,
> may Blessed Ratnasambhava go before me,
> his consort Mamaki behind me;
> help me to cross the bardo's dangerous pathway
> and bring me to the perfect Buddha state."

AH

By saying this inspiration-prayer with deep devotion, he will dissolve into rainbow light in the heart of Blessed Ratnasambhava and his consort, and become a Sambhogakaya Buddha in the southern Realm, The Glorious.

By being shown in this way, liberation is certain, however weak one's capacities may be. Yet even after being shown like this many times, there are people whose good opportunities have run out, such as those who have done great evil or let their samaya practice degenerate, who will not recognize. Disturbed by desire and neurotic veils, they will be afraid of the sounds and lights and will escape, so then on the fourth day Blessed Amitabha's circle of deities will come to invite them, together with the light-path of the hungry ghosts, built from desire and meanness. To show him again, one should call the dead person by name and say these words:

"O son of noble family, listen without distraction. On the fourth day, a red light, the purified element of fire, will shine, and at the same time Blessed Amitabha will appear before you from the red western Realm, The Blissful. His body is red in color, he holds a lotus in his hand and sits on a peacock throne, embracing his consort Pandaravasini. He is accompanied by the two male Bodhisattvas Avalokitesvara and Manjusri and the two female Bodhisattvas Gita and Aloka, so that six Buddha forms appear out of the space of rainbow light.

"The red light of the skandha of perception in its basic purity, the wisdom of discrimination, brilliant red, adorned with discs of light, luminous and clear, sharp and bright, will come from the heart of Amitabha and his consort and pierce your heart so that your eyes cannot bear to look at it. Do not be afraid of it. At the same time, together with the wisdom light, the soft yellow light of the hungry ghosts will also shine. Do not take pleasure in it, give up desire and yearning.

"At that time, under the influence of intense desire, you will be terrified and escape from the sharp, bright red light, but you will feel pleasure and attraction towards the soft yellow light of the hungry ghosts. At that moment do not fear the red light, sharp and brilliant, luminous and clear, but recognize it as wisdom. Let your mind rest in it, relaxed, in a state of non-action. Be drawn to it with faith and longing. If you recognize it as your own natural radiance, even if you do not feel devotion and do not say the inspiration-prayer, all the forms and lights and rays will merge inseparably with you, and you will attain enlightenment. If you cannot recognize it in this way, supplicate it with devotion, thinking, 'It is the light-ray of Blessed Amitabha's compassion, I take refuge in it.' It is the light-ray hook of Blessed Amitabha's compassion. Feel devotion and do not escape. Even if you escape it will stay with you inseparably.

"Do not be afraid, do not be attracted to the soft yellow light of the hungry ghosts. That is the light-path of unconscious tendencies accumulated by your intense desire. If you are attracted to it you will fall into the realm of hungry ghosts, and experience unbearable misery from hunger and thirst. It is an obstacle blocking the path of liberation, so do not be attracted to it, but give up your unconscious tendencies. Do not yearn for it. Feel longing for the luminous, brilliant red light, and say this inspiration-prayer with intense one-pointed concentration on Blessed Amitabha and his consort:

SHA

> When through intense desire I wander in
>   samsara,
> on the luminous light-path of dis-
>   criminating wisdom,
> may Blessed Amitabha go before me,
> his consort Pandaravasini behind me;
> help me to cross the bardo's dangerous
>   pathway
> and bring me to the perfect

Buddha state."

By saying this inspiration-prayer with deep devotion, he will dissolve into rainbow light in the heart of Blessed Amitabha, Infinite Light, with his consort, and become a Sambhokaya Buddha in the western Realm, The Blissful.

It is impossible not to be liberated by this, yet even after being shown in this way, sentient beings cannot give up their unconscious tendencies because of long habituation, and under the influence of envy and evil karma they are afraid of the sounds and lights; they are not caught by the light-ray hook of compassion, but wander downwards to the fifth day of the bardo state. So then Blessed Amoghasiddhi's circle of deities with their light-rays of compassion will come to invite them, and the light-path of the jealous gods, built from the emotion of envy, will also invite them. Then, to show him again, one should call the dead person by name and say these words:

"O son of noble family, listen without distraction. On the fifth day, a green light, the purified element of air, will shine, and at the same time Blessed Amoghasiddhi, lord of the circle, will appear before you from the green northern Realm, Accumulated Actions. His body is green in color, he holds a double vajra in his hand and sits on a throne of shang-shang birds soaring in the sky, embracing his consort Samaya-Tara. He is accompanied by the two male Bodhisattvas Vajrapani and Sarvanivaranaviskambhin and the two female Bodhisattvas Gandha and Naivedya, so that six Buddha forms appear out of the space of rainbow light.

"The green light of the skandha of concept in its basic purity, the action-accomplishing wisdom, brilliant green, luminous and clear, sharp and terrifying, adorned with discs of light, will come from the heart of Amoghasiddhi and his consort and pierce your heart so that your eyes cannot bear to look at it. Do not be afraid of it. It is the spontaneous play of your own mind, so rest in the supreme state free from activity and care, in which there is no near or far, love or hate. At the same time, together with the wisdom light, the soft red light of the jealous gods, caused by envy, will also shine on you. Meditate so that there is no difference between love and hate. But if your intelligence is weak, then simply do not take pleasure in it.

"At that time, under the influence of intense envy, you will be terrified and escape from the sharp, brilliant green light, but you will feel pleasure and attraction towards the soft red light of the jealous gods. At that moment do not be afraid of the green light, sharp and brilliant, luminous and clear, but recognize it as wisdom. Let your mind rest in it, relaxed, in a state of non-action, and supplicate it with devotion, thinking, 'It is the light-ray of Blessed Amoghasiddhi's compassion, I take refuge in it.' It is the light-ray hook of Blessed Amoghasiddhi's compassion, called the action-accomplishing wisdom, so long for it and do not escape. Even if you escape it will stay with you inseparably.

"Do not be afraid of it, do not be attracted to the soft red light of the

SA

jealous gods. That is the inviting path of karma accumulated by your intense envy. If you are attracted to it you will fall into the realm of the jealous gods, and experience unbearable misery from fighting and quarreling. It is an obstacle blocking the path of liberation, so do not be attracted to it, but give up your unconscious tendencies. Feel longing for the luminous, brilliant green light, and say this inspiration-prayer with intense one-pointed concentration on Blessed Amoghasiddhi and his consort:

> When through intense envy I wander in samsara,
> on the luminous light-path of action-accomplishing wisdom,
> may Blessed Amoghasiddhi go before me,
> his consort Samaya-Tara behind me;
> help me to cross the bardo's dangerous pathway
> and bring me to the perfect Buddha state."

By saying this inspiration-prayer with deep devotion, he will dissolve into rainbow light in the heart of Blessed Amoghasiddhi and his consort, and become a Sambhogakaya Buddha in the northern Realm, Perfected Actions.

However weak his good karmic results may be, by being shown like this in many stages, if he does not recognize at one he will at another, so it is impossible not to be liberated. But even after being shown in this way many times, those who have been habituated to many unconscious tendencies for a long time and have never become familiar with the pure visions of the five wisdoms, are carried backwards by their bad tendencies even though they are shown, so that they are not caught by the light-ray hook of compassion, but become bewildered and frightened by the lights and rays, and wander downwards. So then on the sixth day the Buddhas of the five families with their consorts and attendant deities will appear simultaneously, and at the same time the lights of the six realms will also shine simultaneously.

To show him, one should call the dead person by name and say these words:

"O son of noble family, listen without distraction. Even though you were shown when the light of each of the five families appeared until yesterday, under the influence of bad tendencies you were bewildered by them, and so you have remained here until now. If you had recognized the natural radiance of the wisdoms of those five families as your own projection, you would have dissolved into rainbow light in the body of one of the five families and become a Sambhogakaya Buddha, but because you did not recognize you have gone on wandering here until this time. So now watch without distraction.

"Now the five families will appear all together, and what is called the four wisdoms combined will come to invite you; recognize them. O son of noble family, the four colored lights of the four purified elements will shine; at the same time the Buddha Vairocana and his consort will appear just as before from the central Realm, All-pervading Circle; the Buddha Vajrasattva with his consort and attendants will appear from the eastern Realm, Complete Joy; the Buddha Ratnasambhava with his consort and attendants will appear from the southern Realm, The Glorious; the Buddha Amitabha with his consort and attendants will appear from the western Blissful Realm of Lotuses; and the Buddha Amoghasiddhi with his consort and attendants will appear from the northern Realm, Perfected Actions, out of the space of rainbow light.

MA

"O son of noble family, beyond those Buddhas of the five families the wrathful guardians of the gates will also appear: Vijaya, the Victorious; Yamantaka, Destroyer of Death; Hayagriva, the Horse-necked; and Amrtakundali, Coil of Nectar; and the female guardians of the gates: Ankusa, the Hook; Pasa, the Noose; Srnkhala, the Chain; and Ghanta, the Bell. The six sages, the Blessed Ones, will also appear: Indra of the Hundred sacrifices, sage of the gods; Vemacitra, Splendid Robe, sage of the jealous gods; the Lion of the Sakyas, sage of human beings; Dhruvasinha, Steadfast Lion, sage of the animals; Jvalamukha, Flaming Mouth, sage of the hungry ghosts; and Dharmaraja, the Dharma King, sage of the hell-beings. Samantabhadra and Samantabhadri, the All-Good Father and Mother of all the Buddhas, will also appear. These forty-two deities of the Sambhogakaya will emerge from within your own heart and appear before you; they are the pure form of your projections so recognize them.

"O son of noble family, those realms too do not exist anywhere else, but lie in the four directions of your heart with the center as fifth, and now they emerge from within your heart and appear before you. Those images too do not come from anywhere else, but are the primordial spontaneous play of your mind, so recognize them in this way. O son of noble family, those images are neither large nor small, but perfectly proportioned. They each have their own adornments, their costume, their color, their posture, their throne and their symbol. They are spread out in five couples; each of the five is encircled by a halo of the five colored lights. The whole mandala, the male and female deities of the families, will appear completely all at once. Recognize them, for they are your yidams.

"O son of noble family, from the hearts of those Buddhas of the five families and their consorts, the light-rays of the four wisdoms will each shine upon your heart, very fine and clear, like sunbeams stretched out.

"First the wisdom of the dharmadhatu, a cloth of luminous white light-rays, brilliant and terrifying, will shine upon your heart from the heart of Vairocana. In this cloth of light-rays a sparkling white disc will appear, very clear and bright, like a mirror facing downwards, adorned with five discs like itself, ornamented with discs and smaller discs, so that it has no center or circumference.

"From the heart of Vajrasattva, on the luminous blue cloth of the mirror-like wisdom, will appear a blue disc like a turquoise bowl face-downwards, adorned with discs and smaller discs.

"From the heart of Ratnasambhava, on the luminous yellow cloth of the wisdom of equality, will appear a yellow disc like a golden bowl face-downwards, adorned with discs and smaller discs.

"From the heart of Amitabha, on the luminous red cloth of the wisdom of discrimination, will appear a sparkling red disc like a coral bowl face-downwards, shining with the deep light of wisdom, very clear and bright, adorned with five discs like itself, ornamented with discs and smaller discs, so that it has no center or circumference.

"They too will shine upon your heart.

"O son of noble family, these also have arisen out of the spontaneous play of your own mind, they have not come from anywhere else; so do not be attracted to them, do not fear them, but stay relaxed in a state free from thought. In that state all the images and light-rays will merge with you and you will attain enlightenment.

"O son of noble family, the green light of action-accomplishing wisdom does not appear, because the energy of your wisdom is not yet fully matured.

"O son of noble family, this is called the experience of the four wisdoms combined, the passage-way of Vajrasattva. At this time, remember your guru's previous teachings

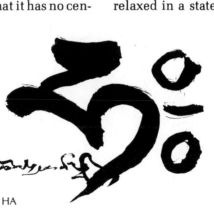

HA

on the showing. If you remember the meaning of the showing you will have faith in your earlier experiences, and so you will recognize them, like the meeting of mother and son or like seeing old friends again. As though cutting off doubt, you will recognize your own projections and enter the pure, changeless path of the dharmata; and through that faith a continuous meditative state will arise, and you will dissolve into the great self-existing form of wisdom and become a Sambhogakaya Buddha who never falls back.

"O son of noble family, together with the wisdom lights, the lights of the impure, illusory six realms will shine: the soft white light of the gods, the soft red light of the jealous gods, the soft blue light of human beings, the soft green light of the animals, the soft yellow light of the hungry ghosts and the soft smoky light of hell-beings. These six will shine together with the pure wisdom lights. At that moment do not grasp or be attracted to any of them, but stay relaxed in a state free from thought. If you are afraid of the pure wisdom lights and attracted to the impure lights of the six realms, you will take on the body of a creature of the six realms, and you will grow weary, for there is never any escape from the great ocean of the misery of samsara.

"O son of noble family, if you have not been shown by a guru's instruction you will be afraid of those images and pure wisdom lights, and attracted to the impure lights of samsara; do not do so, but feel devotion to the pure wisdom lights, sharp and brilliant. Think with devotion, 'The light-rays of the wisdom and compassion of the Blessed Ones, the Buddhas of the five families, have come to seize me with compassion; I take refuge in them.' Do not be attracted to the lights of the six realms of illusion, do not yearn for them, but say this inspiration-prayer with intense one-pointed concentration on the Buddhas of the five families and their consorts:

> When through the five poisons I wander in samsara
> on the luminous light-path of the four wisdoms combined,
> may the conquerors, the five families, go before me,
> the consorts of the five families behind me;
> save me from the light-paths of the six impure realms,
> help me to cross the bardo's dangerous pathway
> and bring me to the five pure Buddha realms.''

By saying this inspiration-prayer, the superior man recognizes his own projections and, merging with non-duality, becomes a Buddha; the average man recognizes himself through intense devotion and attains liberation; even the inferior man prevents rebirth in the six realms by the purifying power of the prayer, and understanding the meaning of the four wisdoms combined, attains enlightenment by the passage-way of Vajrasattva. By being shown clearly and precisely in this way, many sentient beings will recognize and be liberated.

Lion Roars Sun Set Over

This spontaneous linked verse poem was spoken into a tape recorder by Chogyam Trungpa and Allen Ginsberg at 1111 Pearl Street in Boulder, Colorado on August 1, 1974. In this transcription Chogyam Trungpa's lines are set in roman type. *Allen Ginsberg's lines are set in italics.*

In the realm of no-mind
there was Naropa Institute.
Yellow sun fell over Rockies as whispering poets
   completed their thoughts.
Then there was a lion's roar,
which is no mind's claim;
that mind doesn't exist;
but there is still lingering lion's roar
proclaiming Naropa Institute,
in the form of the tiny purring of wheels and
   tracking of manganese oxide across electric
   grids.
Form is empty,
emptiness is form,
therefore we got the birth of the either, neither, or
   the other.

Brushwork by Greg Coffey

Rockies' East Slope

"So no rush," spoke the machine.
Naropa was hassled by an old hag who mocked
   him by saying, "You don't understand the
   meaning behind the words."
By my grey beard the old hag spoke wrong!
Wrongness is old hat as it is,
as it was, as it should be,
as it might be, so forth.
*What would Naropa do with bone and cunt
   thereafter?*
Either the word or sense
which you can't figure out,
he was in trouble,
had to seek Tilopa.
Tilopa in his animal skin solitude was thinking,
thinking nothing,
except eating fish
*which he caught with his bare hands and eyeballs
   by the silvery waterside,*
by the dozen,
and cooked or ate raw;
ate raw,
because that is rawness of life.
Strange sashimi in some mountain nook!
Milking the rock, eating the fire, in order to
   quench your thirst. Tomorrow we visit the freak
   show.
And the fish eyes were stars,
as brilliant as the crescent moon,
which is October 8th day.
Match lit, smoke risen,
turned into clouds,
dissolve like fish powder in the broken mind.
Glorious to be Tilopa,
Glory be to Tilopa!
Glory be to Allen Ginsberg!
Glory be to Chogyam Trungpa!
Glory be to the air conditioner!
Likewise
*in the red suspenders on which everything hangs.
   Yes!*
If there is no Dharma drum
let us beat on the drum of no-Dharma,
which is still the drum of the Dharma.
*And if there's no God, then let's beat
on the height of the gondola!*
Let us proclaim
that —
This! Nothingness! Everything at the same time!
*What will the startled multitudes shriek out in
   their subway slumber?*

They are out in the countryside, where the jungles
   and forests and rocks and stars are immaculate.
*Will they be able to put their 35ᶜ tokens in the
   slot machine if there ain't no God?*
It is possible because of it.
*Will they be able to look at the new lion's eyes in
   the Bronx Zoo if there's no God?*
It is possible because of it.
*Will they be able to sail over the Atlantic in giant
   disappearing ocean liners if there's no God?*
It is possible because of it.
*Will they be able to ascend over the earth in
   silvery spaceships blasting atomic fossil fuel
   behind —*
it
them
is highly possible because of it, my dear.
*Will they be able to — it is highly possible
   because of it, my dear — will they —*
That is questionable sweetheart.
Okay, honey, they will.
Who knows who they are,
what are they?
*They're your-my grandmother with her long pink
   nightie, neatly embroidered at the edges,
   sleeping in her skull in grave lawn —*
They are the people who used to gather together
   in the corral
with the horses, mules, and donkeys
celebrating the end of the War on Times Sq.,
and celebrating the beginning of the War
in Piccadily.
Ties you on hunh.
Fat pussy cream.
Anything you say, sir.
*Even in the darkest jungles of Congo,
or the marketplace at Ulan Bator?*
The darkest of the darkest,
the darkest of the darkest,
the darkest of the darkest,
the darkest of the darkest,
the darkest of the darkest,
THE DARKEST OF THE DARKEST:
delightful because it is so dark;
therefore it is light.
*Coming on in here,
with yer flashlight,
looking for a flask —*
Candle's ring! Hamburger!
*That's what became of the Lion's Roar, a
   hamburger by the saki cupside?*

Saki comes out of the Lion's Roar,
hamburger comes out of the Lion's Roar!
Glorious to be Naropa and his hags!
*But the old tale teller said pure water poured out
of the lion's ear —*
Who knows,
there's mystery in the past.
They say 'twas a man was inspired by a God!
God was inspired by a man
*only repeating old tales told by firelight when
people were scared of the lightning.*
Precisely,
there is lightning because there are dragons,
hurricanes, crocodiles, frogs, lizards, and flies,
*sub-microscopic bacteria ascending kundalini
pathways towards the neckbone.*
There is no neck,
so there is no bone.
*so microscopic galaxies proclaiming their lion
roar —?*
Lion doesn't roar,
that was a joke,
but roar roars the lion.
So microscopic roars produce vast neon lions.
Submachine guns.
*Just all done in the line of duty, sir, said the lion
departing,*
*with his tail wrapped between his legs, slinking
off,*
who knows where.
Let us bring the unicorn along.
*Unicorn objected, "I was the seed of Christ, Son
of the King of Heaven, Lord of the Universe,
ruler of all, central authority, identical with
CIA."*
CIA is a product of mind,
Communist party product of daydream,
product of nightmare.
Look! Look!
The Nazis are coming again?
Is that why there're whispers in the marketplace?
Nazis are Nazis,
they have run out of Jews to persecute.
*Jews have begun the machine gun attack on
Allah.*
Allah is freegul frugal,
parsimonious;
Sufism,
dances a lot,
talks alot,
overflowing with divine love,
to the sweet cistern
which flows to the ocean overhead.
Ocean might be contaminated —

*Vast ocean herself with all her dolphins, whales,
swimming unicorns?*
Maybe this will save —
sick rat is a cunning and a good one,
has beady eyes;
cockroach survives radiation.
Glorious to be them,
free from Sufism, Hinduism, Buddhism,
*free from Chogyam Trungpa, Allen Ginsberg,
President Nixon, and pairs of —*
all the rest of it!
And pairs of eyeglasses!
And all the rest of it!
*Glorious to be the roar of the motorcycle noise
down the dusk street,*
that is the Lion's Roar.
*Glorious to be the beady eyed squirrel, stealing
nuts from the campground!*
Glorious to be the saint,
*Glorious to be a grain of sand, waving its arms in
the desert;*
By trying to be one,
exploring thousands means,
by a thousand means,
flopping into one.
One doesn't produce zero,
One began the goy —
one begins anything you want,
one began Jupiter;
one begins anything you want,
*one begins the squeal of lizards, swimming in the
ocean frost;*
one begins anything you want,
one begins vast scaley fishlike dinosaurs;
one begins anything you want,
*one begins the nimbus after clear days, rainless
months;*
one begins anything you want,
but one doesn't exist.
One therefore begins the full moon,
crescent moon, on the 8th day of the lunar
calendar.
*On 8th day lunar calendar what monster was
born?*
*What being was born, if you prefer me there?
Buddha?*
hum. . . .
Cause I don't know the reference, that's why —
Person with no tail,
no hair on his chest, but brilliant eyes
which look at you.
*Person with spine and big feet approaching you,
with open hand,*
carrying a sceptre,

crowned with water garlands,
shivering with nervousness,
stammering, embarrassed by elephants,
now that he or you conquered the world,
swept under the dustbin cabinet with the starving
 mice.
The mice shit beautifully,
in beautiful pellets,
the cat smells hungrily round the garage door.
They have flying cats
here, the unicorns waving the iridescent feathers,
fitting the encyclopedia and dictionary with
 lights,
large, gawky professorial tomes with long
 tongues,
and beady eyeglasses,
and the appearance of living dress.
Glorious to be lack, lack of love,
Glorious to be beady eyed, ratnosed professors of
 mental technology,
on their way to the jail,
the plane money in their pockets, to say goodbye.
Their deceptions are too cute,
but they got a good lawyer,
their lies too self spoken,
and the lawyer recognizes them, nullity of the
 judge,
tongue twister,
speechmaker,
crocodile,
good man to have if you have a murder rap,
alligatorial smile,
all televised before the public with great solemn
 conventional debate,
shedding the crocodilean tears,
fell down to the crocodilean shoes.
Argentina,
the Argentinean yogi!
More walk gently,
a child shoed softly,
a white dragon is no offense,
stinging monster with pleasure, gunslinger,
kindness is no offense,
no horror zoo, in the fence.
"I can" is regarded as reminder to —
because it says think and please,
before and after.
Typhon bows and scrapes at the door.
Your house is burned;
What shall we do?
said the whirlwind rushing up with showers of
 water.
Fire Department's inadequate!
Call in the National Guardian Angels!

What nationality are we?
Perfect Planetarian.
What planet are we in?
The place where we're sitting.
Where are we sitting?
1111 Pearl Street, at Naropa Institute.
Call them up!
You mean the sun? Each Sunbeam? No
 telephones in that atmosphere. . .
Really?
We'll leave them alone.
Let 'em sleep.
How about the stars?
Stars — got work to do.
How about the mosquitoes
buzzing around our ears?
They are a helpful sign.
How about the secretary?
She types with tattoo-like fingers, like proboscis of
 tiny winged anvils, entering the skin.
Maybe the secretary might perspire,
and she might change her gearshift.
Maybe crocodile tears aspire to Lion's Roar —
Lion's Roar —
good for you,
let us proclaim Lion's Roar;
But will we include lion's jaw that bites us so
 hard, to the death?
Can't, they're in your ears, lion's loudness,
 without getting near the toothsome cage.
The work in London is full of Vicarity
hard enough for rubber booted climbers to rejoice
 on
. . . soaked in blood,
eaten by a Rocky Mountain coyote.
Loud wails in the moonlight as the predators get
 their dangling fix!
My manuscript is disorder,
my mind perfectly clear,
My work is no work,
but a worklessness;
my play makes the iron cow sweat.
Shall we push the red button?
It was pushed, sire, aeons ago.
How about pushing this snow mountain and this
 red button?
How about pushing the roof?
Glories be to it,
Glorious to be its.
The anger can't be defined,
Nor need be pronounced, nor worried about,
 anymore —
Thank you.

from Fast Speaking Woman

I'm a shouting woman
I'm a speech woman
I'm an atmosphere woman
I'm an airtight woman
I'm a flesh woman
I'm a flexible woman
I'm a high heeled woman
I'm a high style woman
I'm an automobile woman
I'm a mobile woman
I'm an elastic woman
I'm a necklace woman
I'm a silk scarf woman
I'm a know nothing woman
I'm a know it all woman

I'm a day woman
I'm a doll woman
I'm a sun woman
I'm a late afternoon woman
I'm a clock woman
I'm a wind woman

I'M A SILVER LIGHT WOMAN
I'M AN AMBER LIGHT WOMAN
I'M AN EMERALD LIGHT WOMAN

I'm an abalone woman
I'm the abandoned woman
I'm the woman abashed, the gibberish woman
the aborigine woman, the woman absconding
the absent woman
the transparent woman
the absinthe woman
the woman absorbed, the woman under tyranny
the contemporary woman, the mocking woman
the artist dreaming inside her house!

I'm the diaphonous woman
I'm the diamond light woman
I'm the adamant woman

                              flowers that clean
                              water that cleans
                              flowers that clean as I go

I'm a bird woman
I'm a book woman
I'm a devilish clown woman
I'm a holy clown woman
I'm a whirling dervish woman
I'm a playful light woman
I'm a fast speaking woman

                              — Anne Waldman

Salina Star Route

tonight
    the sky
        is of great fragility
    as I fall into my hands
          the stars
go in and out of their bodies
        cued
by the hollow calls
      of nightbirds
        stirring
in the silver light
    the stars
      exiting
      and returning
        on
the arms
    of the dark mountain
      sexual shawl
    holding me
in its deepest curve
      mother's letter
demanding attention
      unknown sister
       ancient lover
soft blood
    fold in which I flutter like a god

here the brook which has held snow
    or dry grass
        all
        winter lay
    against the house
      the small space
in the deep
    cleft
    shaggy shelter
    flank
      of the eating
      necessities
        etched
under the stars
    made lighter by them
        now
flows!
    to the creek
      down the canyon
out spreading
    into the flat lap
      of the plains

this dark has flowers
        white
            with a silvery
                    purple stem
awaiting the sluggish bees
                threatening
all else
        with their assertive purpose
                    this dark
has black squirrels
          sleeping
                spending winter
for the night
        close
           on the orange bark
                  and mice
moving like tawny blurs
          grain balls
          along the openings
                  peering out
at me
        becoming familiar
               with my habits
                    dark
cottonwood
neither dead
        nor living
              a place for nests
a place
        for the bluejay's greyish crest
to flash
        in the early
             green morning
tall
    mountain tree drinking
                freely
of this dark
and now the moon is rising
        and now
             on the other side of the road
the creek rushes
        steady and
             bold from the many brooks
artery
        of chill metal veins
             curling around
the abandoned
        mines.

before sleep
        move in the soft hair of the night
comb

                      through the clutching
                                          juniper
let
      young willowy firs
                              brush me
                                            play me
out into
              their web of no distinction
                                          useful
only as statement
                          the real plans
                                      are already
in the oil company's drawer

and now I drink a cup of tea

                                          — *Sidney Goldfarb*

Poem on Plane — 7/18/74 6:50 PM MDST

Now I know what they mean by the Great Plains!

Flat to the horizon in patterns of
                    tan & brown & green
but up ahead toward Denver
        the mountains abruptly rise

There's a rainstorm over there
        between us & the mountains
as we quickly now descend
            to land in Denver

Lightning!

                                          — *Jackson Mac Low*

Naropa

late night porch dinners
endless dharma debate
Rinpoche no promise lecture
where let go — legs?
small of back?

— *Diane Di Prima*

July 29 1974 Lecture by Rinpoche

Panics are a source of happiness.
You find yourself roasted inside out.
The teacher and the students panic.
Think twice! As you reconsider the world it will be a better world.
The teacher is also naked. The teacher is the conductor of your enlightenment.
Some people decide to wear a top some people decide not to wear a top.
   Mostly all wear bottom.
It's not one-pointed energy, it's all over the place.
Power dash energy.
Power comes first. Energy exists!
The point of chauvinism is problem!
You can become goodly crazy
   or badly crazy.
No no. Just panicking we go back and forth and forth and back!
Only thing I can say is don't panic, but don't stop panicking.
Shit on teacher's rug and recline.

Notes by Alex Di Prima — age 10

He Does Not
Give the Reader
One Line of Information

The dragon
of chaos proceeds
finding gold earth
stars. Alchemical
bottles of Guiness
Stout sprout
eating chocolate
fish under
the soothing
moon and astronauts.

Alex Di Prima — age 10

This Prairie Dog

This prairie dog is Buddha
   come down for all to see.
This prairie dog is Buddha
   coming for his 1005th life.
What more could he do for me & you?
How would you know him? Well
He is in the form of a fat prairie dog
   sitting zazen!

Mini Di Prima
(written at age 8)

The End of the Land as Woman

the sea   the green hair
the land wrapped around
her coleander heart

no the shores of her chamber
no the whorls

of ash in brooklyn ash in the eyes
cinders on the bare feet —

she somewhere
in the trance ported from the east
san francisco

she bearing 2 children
just like that
romulus and remus

she with billowed folds in the dress of
ambergris and salt

no matter how she turns
there can be no bright rose
in ambergris but faint perfume

she penitent
against the world those shadows
the girth of treesway
and the tongs of her repentance
the coal of her ovum thoughts
her broad thoughts
where the world builds 1,2,3

she the music of ocean's dense pitch
she the beach where ocean rests
a crushed wing on sands
on the dense belly resting
notches in the furrows of her hair

she with muscle the fiber of limb's knotted wood
she of bilegreen eyes who would eat
our lives scatter our teeth to the wind to the north
to the west where her breast heaves pacifica

she without stain blameless
cruel as 2 languages
known to neither ear

— Jim Burbank

from Subduing Demons in America

everyone
is laughing
at you
everyone is laughing
at you
and making
fun
of you
and making fun
of you
and making fun of you,
they're drunk
and stoned
and nasty
they're drunk and stoned
and nasty
they're drunk and stoned and nasty,
and you're surrounded
and you're surrounded
by this terrifying
freak
show
and you're surrounded by this terrifying
freak show
by this terrifying freak show,
and they're ridiculing
you
and they're ridiculing you
and they're ridiculing you
and laughing
at you
and laughing at you
and laughing at you,
and you're
uptight
and you're uptight
and you're uptight
and you're really
tight
and you're really tight
and you're really tight,
and you try

everyone
is laughing
at you
everyone is laughing
at you
and making
fun
of you
and making fun
of you
and making fun of you,
they're drunk
and stoned
and nasty
they're drunk and stoned
and nasty
they're drunk and stoned and nasty,
and you're surrounded
and you're surrounded
by this terrifying
freak
show
and you're surrounded by this terrifying
freak show
by this terrifying freak show,
and they're ridiculing
you
and they're ridiculing you
and they're ridiculing you
and laughing
at you
and laughing at you
and laughing at you,
and you're
uptight
and you're uptight
and you're uptight
and you're really
tight
and you're really tight
and you're really tight,
and you try
to smile

to smile
and you try to smile
and you try to smile,
but you can't
but you can't
but you can't,
and you can't
think
of anything
to say
to say
to anyone
and you can't think of anything to say
to anyone
to anyone,
and nobody
will talk
to you
and nobody will talk
to you
and nobody will talk to you,
and you are confused
and lonely
and unhappy
and freaked out
and you are confused
and lonely and unhappy
and freaked out
and you are confused and lonely
and unhappy and freaked out,
and you just
want
to touch
somebody
and you just want
to touch somebody
and you just want to touch somebody,
but you've forgotten
how
to do it
but you've forgotten
how to do it
but you've forgotten how to do it,
and you just
want
and you just want

and you try to smile
and you try to smile,
but you can't
but you can't
but you can't,
and you can't
think
of anything
to say
to say
to anyone
and you can't think of anything to say
to anyone
to anyone,
and nobody
will talk
to you
and nobody will talk
to you
and nobody will talk to you,
and you are confused
and lonely
and unhappy
and freaked out
and you are confused
and lonely and unhappy
and freaked out
and you are confused and lonely
and unhappy and freaked out,
and you just
want
to touch
somebody
and you just want
to touch somebody
and you just want to touch somebody,
but you've forgotten
how
to do it
but you've forgotten
how to do it
but you've forgotten how to do it,
and you just
want
and you just want
and you just want

and you just want   to hold
to hold   somebody
somebody   to hold somebody
to hold somebody   to hold somebody,
to hold somebody,   and kiss
and kiss   somebody
somebody   and kiss somebody
and kiss somebody   and kiss somebody,
and kiss somebody,   and you want
and you want   to do it
to do it   and you want to do it
and you want to do it   and you want to do it,
and you want to do it,   and you are living
and you are living   and you are living
and you are living   in an airport
in an airport   in an airport
in an airport,   in a Holiday
in a Holiday   Inn
Inn   in a Holiday Inn,
in a Holiday Inn,   in a Ford
in a Ford   Pinto
Pinto   in a Ford Pinto,
in a Ford Pinto,   in a Dodge
in a Dodge   truck
truck   in a Dodge truck,
in a Dodge truck,   in a television
in a television   set
set   in a television set
in a television set   in a television set,
in a television set,   and the Ajax
and the Ajax   woman
woman   and the Ajax woman
and the Ajax woman   is scrubbing
is scrubbing   away
away   is scrubbing away
is scrubbing away   at your heart
at your heart   and the Ajax woman is scrubbing away
and the Ajax woman is scrubbing away   at your heart
at your heart   at your heart,
at your heart,   until
until   there is nothing
there is nothing   left
left   to work with
to work with   and there is nothing left
and there is nothing left   to work with
to work with   and there is nothing left to work with,
and there is nothing left to work with,   and whatever
and whatever   is left
is left   and whatever is left
and whatever is left   and whatever is left,
and whatever is left,   just goes
just goes   down
down   the drain
the drain   just goes
just goes   down the drain
down the drain   just goes down the drain
just goes down the drain

— *John Giorno*

Boulder Blues

We are here to disappear

ripples
waves
buttes
ridge
gulleys
guts

flint & metal sparking constantly
no more presumptuous than wind in the leaves

— *Anne Waldman*

Syllogism

for Frederick

when the legs of my words
hug you
it is love

when
allowed to come,
the poem

what makes a mind
receive its dragon
biting tail

is boredom —
a book of leaves
a home

seeing is love
a head before the tail
sees behind

I love you.
wild horses
mirrors

so words
reflect the lay
of the line

in the light
letting two go
lets one

word a hand
a hot woman
tenders

teach us

— *Sara Vogeler*

Bacchae Sonnet 7

the word Mind the word path the word protection
the word word make yourself suitable
the word the-radiant-light the word one-valueness
the word to-set-the-whole-of-reality-into-motion
the word inseparable-from, the word gnash
the words döchag shidang timu make yourself
this osmosis-being transform cancer tissue transform greed the hate that delusion of Fury in the outer field

the word Nothing flowers where the word cunt's
the word cock help me with my words
say the sentient women the sentient men
I oppress I'm oppressed o this fucked-up lurching between.
nothing but the slaver of the sick worry, the sick
abstract worry in the Road games, tongue maggots travel in
tomorrow Jan. 22nd rapid opinions opinions from yesterday the 20th,
I've lost this tissue-knowledge of my today's pain again, again
there's no *this* day, Jan. 21st; make yourself suitable

—*Armand Schwerner*

Che Bodhisattva

The body of the revolution
burned before the millions
the color of wet earth shining
could see within it
their own eyes staring back
secrets they do not want
us to ask
      the dead
body of the revolution betrayed in
the jungle, the body that fell
into a mouth of hungry cities
chewing the light, o body
of a million eyes
seeing the world all at once
while feeding it your lives.

— Rick Fields

The Four Laws of Thermodynamics

Rules in Salinas

We Reserve the Right to refuse to sell chips
to anyone and to cash anyone out at any time.

No Misdeals.

If you pass you cannot raise.

Protect your Own hand.

— Lewis Mac Adams

SOMAONEIRIKA 3   *The Parabolic Path of the Stone*

(for Raquel Jodorowsky)

I am walking along a path watching the trees.
There is some sort of round object
up in the tree on my left.
Or else the object is between *two* trees.
And as I look at this curious object I see
it is like bundled up newspaper
enclosing a basketball, or perhaps a hunk
of stone — a round stone, a large round stone,
perhaps it is a largish, volleyball size, spherical
stone. Perhaps it is a polished lump of turquoise.
Or a lapis lazuli bowling ball that has veered
off course of its Siberian lane
that ends with ten bright red fly agarics.
Or a ball of jade that on close inspection
is not a ball, but the Vajra, the
Diamond that cuts with the sound of thunder,
being visualized and projected at this
very moment in the
hidden hills of Tibet. Now we see it,
now we don't. Crrrack
and it changes continent: milky moonstone
of Brazil, the fractured flesh
of the half-blind white dolphin of the Amazon
in perpetual correspondence with the White Goddess
as Luna descends into the Stone
and we place it like a jewel
on the bosom of our woman
to heal her.
            If so, this
is a rite of healing.
And so, walking along this path, seeing
some sort of object up a tree on my left
or between two trees — and so it is, and it's
wrapped in paper, and can't be seen.
I look closer: it seems these two trees are
leaning together, and they're pushing their branches
upward, and it looks like they're trying to get this
immense seed up higher, and they're pushing and
pushing and getting it up higher, and as I watch them
performing thus, I began to wonder, what *are* they
doing? And no sooner have I thought this when
the object falls at my feet.
Or maybe they threw it.
Or maybe they fumbled it
and lost their treasure of Andes jade.
Or maybe they mistook me for the wandering Lama
in the hills near San Augustin, Colombia,

and that I would take it on to Lima, to the door
of Raquel Jodorowsky, and there reveal
the secret:
                    That a marvelous star
has long sent its marvelous beam
to the Himalayas, where it entered the heads
of men. But that time is no more,
for now it goes to the Andes, to enter
the heads of women.
                              I bend down and pick up
the object. It's like a bag of stone.
Something light, like turquoise.
Or else a large seed wrapped in newspaper.
And I wonder: Should I toss it back?
Will it startle them, this uncanny levitation?
Did the eyeless god of the tree know
of my approach? Is this some dendritic version
of Morse Code, or, better, what was heard
by radio pioneers Marconi and Tesla, signals
from another world, 1900, it said
perhaps: *One . . . Two . . . Three . . .*
one day to reach Four, — when we've learned of
Five —
            So I have this object in my hands
and I've grown tired of wondering about arboreal motives
and I've grown curious about the contents
and I turn my attention completely to the thing itself
and I fold back the paper, each turn like a loop
of Venusian yoni, each a stage of the abalone cunnus
or a lid of the inwardly folding eye —
                                        The thought
crosses my mind: Stone — the kind I
am thinking is extraterrestrial, origin
unknown — Tektite? Perhaps. Brownish green glass,
eyes of Tara — found chiefly in Czechoslovakia
(murals of Castle Karlstejn), Bali and Australian
dreamtime, Texas and Georgia — I think: White
Oak, Jekyll Island, the Marshes of Glynn — every
one a possible site, any one could be the mother
of this object I have in my hands . . .
                                        It is time
to open this sleeping flower,
I am thinking, and reach toward the mystery, when
I feel the vines taking hold of my ankles, O
dark night of the secret Mohave, O that
I could find my hidden dogtail as counter-
twist, anti-torque,
gearshift—   I let go
and it could have been molten stone
for all I know, so brief
was its contact with my flesh.

— *George Quasha*

Photo by Ellen Pearlman

"First Thought, Best Thought"

Allen Ginsberg

from the Spiritual Poetics *class,*

July 29, 1974

I was thinking of something Robert Duncan told me in '63, when I was singing Hare Krishna. He found that I was using my voice and my body a lot more thick and a lot more involved than I was when I was reading poetry. That I was putting more force and more energy and more conviction into the physical rendering of the mantras than I was into what I was supposed to be good at, which was the poetry. Which I think was a real criticism, a seed that stuck a long time and flowered, because from then on I realized, for one thing, that singing is a really good thing, if it can bring that out, and break the shyness or the barrier of fear of energy, or fear of expression. But also it made me conscious of the fact that whatever really great poetry I wrote, like "Howl" or "Kaddish," I was actually able to chant, and use my whole body, whereas in lesser poetry, I wasn't, I was talking. Or, I shouldn't say lesser, but poetry that didn't involve me as much; so in that sense, lesser. So from that point of view, poetry becomes less intellectual or verbal and also becomes a physiological thing. Something where you actually *use* your body, use your breath, use your full breath. At least

chant becomes that — and poetry can approach chant, or poetry when you're really into it can become an expression of the whole body, "single body, single mind," with real *oomph*, as distinct from the practice of poetry as it was all along in my day and probably yours still, which is more of a tentative thing where you're dealing with flimsy materials of your own mind and so you're not really sure whether you should lay it out solid like a prophet, or whether it's worth shouting or speaking or howling, or using your whole self in. That's not, of course, the only form of poetry, because there's a quiet conversational poetry, and there's a whispered poetry, and I guess whispered transmissions even, but that area of full energy is very rarely appreciated now. It's appreciated when you hear it; when you hear it in Dylan, it's totally appreciated, which is the great thing about Dylan — he puts his whole lung in one vowel: "How does it *FEEL*," or as in old blues, "HOME, I'm going HOME," so you have the whole body into it because what is meant is something very definite emotionally, rather than tentative.

So, it's good then to link poetics with some

form of vocalization. Also, I began the class today, somewhat thoughtlessly, shrewdly, with vocalizing, so we're all vocalizing together with some spirit. And in a way, it would be ideal if the poetry we arrive at by writing could involve us joyfully, "lively," — could involve us enough so that we could recite our own poetry with the same kind of spirit as we sing. We sing kind of abandoned — we could dig our poetry as much, actually dig our own utterances. As much as we do our own nonsensicals, our chanting. It's a state that I've sort of arrived at over the years with my own poetry, and I've seen other poets arrive at also. I think it's a good deal, a good thing to keep in mind, because otherwise you get immediately the danger of bawling out bullshit or reciting in a high cracked, tense, nervous voice or a tearful voice, an over tearful voice, or over sentimental, tearful voice. Reciting, "Bullshit, the police are after me, my best friend was busted, where are all the roses?" Which was typical of the poetry of the early 60's. Overgeneralized, but shouted.

So that's the obvious danger, but if you noticed, the voice came somewhere from the top of the throat rather than the center of the body. That's another interesting technical matter for voice, for the vocalization of poetry — that the best poets I've heard, orators, say, do speak from their whole body. Someone who commands attention and authority — it's a very subtle thing, it's not so much what they're saying, it's that the voice does come from the center of the body, from say the heart chakra, which is a learnable thing. I mean, it's something that's developable, when you become conscious of it, when you do a lot of chanting. I think it develops naturally when you solidify and mature.

So there's vocalization, but to have vocalization, you've got to have vowels, vowels make the vocalization easy. You've got something to vocalize, with a vowel you can use your whole lung. What is that called technically? The assonance. The repeated musical use of vowels. Which they also used to teach, but they didn't teach how much fun it is, or they didn't teach that it was a form of yoga, or maybe they did, but I wasn't listening. People who are mentally hung up on what they are saying, and too careful in what they are saying, and not relying enough on their body and spontaneous mind, generally fail to appreciate the solidity and strength of their own organ-like tones, and fail to appreciate that they can really swing with vowels also. Because if you want to give yourself something to work with, poetically, while writing, just remember "a, e, i, o, u, — a, e, i, o, u," or any variation of the vowels.

And for that, if you look at any of the great classic poetic war-horses, like "The Bells" or Shelley's "Adonais" or Shelley's "Epipsychidion" or *Paradise Lost* — a lot of really interesting vibrant, vibratory, stanzaic poetry or blank verse — you find that it's really solid chunks of vowels that you can get your glottis into, or whatever vowels issue from. One that my father taught me when I was young — some lines from Book I in *Paradise Lost*: ". . . Him the Almighty Power/Hurled headlong flaming from the ethereal sky/With hideous ruin and combustion down/To bottomless perdition, there to dwell/In adamantine chains and penal fire,/Who durst defy the Omnipotent to arms." It was just a great voice exercise. I didn't see it as such, I just saw it as a great streak of bopping, I guess. I never saw my father come on like that, you know, with such great vocal fire, vocal force, with such breath — I mean it was nice to see my father so *animated*. Is there a relationship between the root word of "animated" and "breath"? I guess "soul" and the breath links up there somewhere. Soul is breath, in a way, they say.

The title of this course is *Spiritual Poetics*, which was just a spontaneous title arrived at when we had to have a title, but might as well be used. We're beginning with considerations of breath, considerations of vowel, and relation between vowel and intelligence, vowel and soul, — and how these are connected to the breath. As here, say with Chogyam's teaching, "Ah" is a basic mantra — "Ah" as the exhalation of the breath, as appreciation of the breath also. Appreciation of the empty space into which breath flows. The *open* space, into which breath flows.

So if we're talking poetics, and beginning with breath, the vowel road is connected then with the title of the course, *Spiritual Poetics*. And the mantric aspects are a lot more important than has been understood in western poetry — as pure breath, as exhalation of breath, as articulation of breath, as manifestation of breath, as animation, as expression in really the easiest and most natural way of your own nature, which is by breathing, and making a sound while breathing. Just like the wind makes a sound in the leaves. No more presumptuous than the wind in the leaves. Of course, no more honorable either. But at any rate, not guilty. No more guilty than the wind in the leaves. So if you take that approach, that your singing or your chanting or your poetics is as neutral, impersonal, and objective as the wind through the black oak leaves, then you wouldn't have to be ashamed of expressing yourself, because it's not yourself, it's just the wind, it's just wind, it's just breath going through you. Then you might take the trouble to fit it to whatever your subjective intellect is thinking about at the moment, and you might take the trouble to link that breath up with whatever is going on in your mind at the moment, or to what you remember is going on in your mind or your body at the moment. But that can be done as spontaneously as breathing, in the sense that the mind is always working — it's hard to stop, as those of you who have been meditating know.

How many here sit? So, nearly everybody. So we all know the experience of observing our minds moving and listening to chatter and gossip, discursive thought, not being able to stop, and maybe not even needing to attempt to stop it, simply observing it. I've lately come to think of poetry as the possibility of simply articulating that, in other words, observing your mind, remembering maybe one or two thoughts back and laying it out. So in that sense it's as easy as breathing because all you're doing is listening to particulars, those particulars of what you were just thinking about. And in that respect, it's very close to meditation. Meditation is good practice for poetry. In other words, it's not the opposite, it's not an enemy of poetry. It was formerly seen to be, occasionally, by various hung-up intellectuals, who were afraid that they'd be silent, and they wouldn't be able to be poets then. But actually all it does is give you lots of space and place in time to recollect what's going on in your mind, so providing lots of material, lots of ammunition, lots of material to work with.

So if you are practicing in the line of Gertrude Stein and Kerouac, spontaneous transcription, transmission of your thought, how do you choose then what thoughts to put down? The answer is that you don't get a chance to choose because everything's going so fast. So it's like driving on a road; you just have to follow the road. And take turns, "eyeball it," as a carpenter would say. You don't have any scientific measuring rod, except your own mind, really. I don't know of any scientific measuring rod that's usable. So you just have to chance whatever you can and pick whatever you can. So there's also a process of automatic selection. Whatever you can draw in your net is it, is what you got — whatever you can remember, and whatever you can manage physically to write down is your poem, or is your material. And you've got to trust that, sort of as the principle of selection, so you have to be a little athletic about that, in the sense of developing *means* of transcription, ease of transcription, overcoming resistance to transcription.

(Question from class): *Does that also have to do with what you choose to use, either typing, or writing, or tape recorder?*

Yeah, very much so. I want to go into that anyway, in just a minute. First I want to get to the nub of selection, because that used to be a big academic argument about the principle of selectivity and of beatnik writers being unselective, and that selection was so important, that you really had to make fine distinctions between different kinds of thoughts and only choose the loftiest thoughts, or the most poetic thoughts, and you had to intercede or intervene in your mind with another mind from somewhere else, someone else's mind really, Lionel Trilling's mind or Allen Tate's mind, or Brooks and Warren's mind, the critics' minds. You had to use somebody else's mind or some objective mind to choose among the thoughts, but I think that's too hard, I think that's too much work. It'll only get you tangled up in a feedback loop of some sort, because you forget what you were thinking, and you'll think what you were supposed to be thinking. So the problem is to stay with what you were really thinking instead of what you think you're supposed to be thinking.

So from that point of view, I would say that the only thing you can get down is what you can remember and what you can write down. In other words, the actual process of writing, the physical process of writing or vocalizing or tape-recording or babbling spontaneously. That physical activity determines what gets laid out on the paper or on the air. It's a pretty good critic, because the mind somehow or other, if you leave it alone a little bit and accept it, tends to select its own society, tends to cling to obsessions and preoccupations. Recurrent thoughts

Photo by Chuck Stein

finally do get out, things that are really recurrent do come up and are rememberable. And one really difficult part is that there's a tendency toward censorship. That some thoughts seem too embarrassing, too raw, too naked, too irrelevant, too goofy, too personal, too revealing, too damaging to one's own self-image, too cranky, too individualistic, too specialized, or too much fucking your mother or something, so that you don't want to put it down. That's a real problem with everybody, including myself. The *pudeur*, modesty, shyness — like I failed to write down a dream the other day. Fortunately, I remembered it — I saw Peter Orlovsky catch me smoking, and he's very much anti-smoking. We were living together, and in the dream he was so dismayed that he vomited up his liver, and I realized that I was really violating something

sacrosanct and rooted, physiologically rooted in him, in something real. And I got so scared of the domestic situation that I didn't write the dream down. But it was actually one of the more interesting dream-poem possibilities that I'd had in the last month.

But in the moment of writing, there'll be all sorts of images rise, "thinks," separate "thinks" that will be unappetizing, and I think that's the most important part. The parts that embarrass you the most are usually the most interesting poetically, are usually the most naked of all, the rawest, and goofiest, and strangest and most eccentric and at the same time, most representative, most universal, because most individual, most particular, most specific, vomiting out a piece of liver, specific situation, smoking. Actually, I thought that was really just my scene, but really it's universal, it's an archetype, as much as anything's an archetype. And that was something I learned from Kerouac, which was that spontaneous writing could be embarrassing, or could seem to be embarrassing. So the cure for that is to write things down which you will not publish and which you won't show people. To write secretly, to write for nobody's eye, nobody's ear but your own, so you can actually be free to say anything that you want. In other words, it means abandoning being a poet, abandoning any careerism, abandoning even the idea of writing any poetry, really abandoning, giving up as hopeless — abandoning the possibility of really expressing yourself to the nations of the world. Abandoning the idea of being a prophet with honour and dignity, and abandoning the glory of poetry and just settling down in the muck of your own mind. And the way that's practiced is that you take it out a week later and look at it. It's no longer embarrassing, it seems by that time funny. The blood has dried, sort of. So you really have to make a resolution just to write for yourself, but really for yourself, in the sense of no bullshit to impress others, in the sense of not writing poetry to impress yourself, but just writing what yourself is saying.

My own experience with "Howl" was precisely that. After writing some very formalistic poetry, I decided I'd let loose whatever I wanted to let loose with and say what I really had on my mind and not write a poem, finally — break my own forms, break my own ideals, ideas, what I was supposed to be like as a poet and just write whatever I had in mind. And once written, I realized it could never be published, because it would offend too many people, I thought, particularly my family. Which I think is a problem Kerouac had too. He was afraid his mother would read his secret thoughts and disapprove of his friends, or sexual activities, or dope-smoking or beatnik habits, or something — the drinking, who knows, the snot, his masturbation, whatever.

It's a common occurrence, especially among younger poets, to find that the form of writing that they didn't conceive of as their main thing, their main *schtick*, their main poem — like notes to themselves, or their journal, or letters or just sort of banjo-chanting by themselves, or chanting to themselves while walking across Brooklyn Bridge, or on mountaintops — was ac-

tually more interesting, later on, than the stuff they prepared as poetry. And I found that in my case to be so. For years I wrote very formal rhymed verse, and at the same time was keeping a very loose, erratic journal, very similar to a journal that I published called *Indian Journals*. A journal which I've kept continually from '46 on. And I found that little fragments from the journal were more hot than anything I'd written down or prepared and rhymed and poetised with the idea of writing poetry. So it's almost like if you can catch yourself not writing poetry, but writing down what you're really thinking, actually, you arrive at a genuine piece of writing, of self-expression. And that may be more interesting than what you're careeristically considering as your poem. So one of the technical aids would be to stick to poems that you're not going to publish, so that you're really free to write down what you want to write.

(Question): *Do you find that even transcribing straight thoughts tends to focus your attachment to your thoughts?*
What do you mean focus your attachment?

I found that in keeping a journal, I got so attached to thoughts, so aware of thoughts, that I actually was subtly manufacturing more of them to make a more pleasing journal.
Yeah, well, there's a certain amount of baroque elegance that can be indulged in — playfulness — if it's playful enough it's all right. Sometimes. That's just sheer abundance, and playfulness, but while you're doing that, sometimes there's something else going on, an undertow of real thought that you've got to pay attention to. So maybe you start getting baroque, and then interrupt it — just break it off in the middle, be playful and break it off in the middle. William Carlos Williams used a dot for an unfinished sentence, for an unfinished thought — a dot extended out, like a period, but in the middle of a line. Or a dash could be used, as Hart Crane did in a really interesting poem which you might look up, "Havana Rose," which was like a drunken suicide note to himself. It was one of the things that turned me on to raw thought as poetry. A little free-associational piece, like the kind of note you might write to yourself drunk. Which wasn't meant as a poem, which was recovered from his papers, and which is one of his most charming, personal pieces.

How do you use those fragments of thoughts as material — what are you using them as material for?

They're the poem. You don't have to work any more on it. That's it. You don't have to do any more work. No, the whole process of poetry is totally without any work at all. It should be, I think. At least to *begin* with. There might be some work later on, but until you establish this basis of honesty, I don't think it's worth working on anything beyond that. It takes a lot of practice just to get down what you've got. You can worry about it later. I mean it's really so charming and hard. I mean I can't do it that often, actually *catch* myself and write it down. You can't do it once a day or once every week, or once a month even, *really* catch yourself thinking something interesting. Then if you can do one little four-line fragment a month, you've got it made for the rest of your life, you realize, you'd do better than Sappho. As *much* as Sappho, as much as Anacreon. Actually if you're young when you start out, just four lines a month and you've built up a total body of work by the end of your lifetime. You're too much to read. And you can do five minutes a day, practicing five minutes a day, writing, oddly enough, more than anybody wants to read.

Does that mean catching yourself as interesting?

Well, interesting because clear, because definite, because there, because you really did catch yourself. Unwittingly catch yourself. In a moment you didn't quite like, or maybe did like a lot. So that brings up, how do you catch yourself? And how to be prepared to catch yourself. Which brings up the question about materials. What you use for transcription. What I use basically is this pocket notebook. Generally, I use maybe one a month, or one every two months. Twenty-nine cents and a nineteen cent ball point pen, the only investment you need. That's for moving around, for traveling, for getting thoughts on the wing. "Dinosaur, cancer, Buchenwald, hellrat, heavy meadow, sweet oleanders down the middle of the strip of the freeway." Well, that was part of a conversation with Gary Snyder. And the title is, "On the way to pick up Peter in the Sacramento airport," or "I'm going to pick up Peter Sacto Airport." June 1 — not much of an entry.

During meditating, do you ever stop and jot down some of the neat things that happen?

Well, sometimes I take my notebook to meditation and I sneak in a couple of lines or go to the bathroom. I was in Wyoming at the seminary sitting for three months, from September to December last year, and I had the little notebook and a couple of times I interrupted the sitting to write something down. Neruda had died — I had read it in the paper before I went in to sit, and I was thinking about breathing, and — "Some breath breathes out Atlantis, Adonais, some breath breathes out bombs, and dog barks, some breath breathes over Rendezvous Mountain, some breath breathes not at all." I thought, "Gee, that's funny, Neruda's not breathing, so breath breathes not at all." It was so mysterious and strange, that thought, that I pulled out my notebook and wrote it. It's enough. It sat there — and that was the end of my thought. So if I wanted another poem, another thought would be another poem. And that was a very definite end. I mean, what else, you can't go on from there. So breath breathes not at all.

Do you think it's possible to go back to something you wrote earlier?

I don't know if you could intentionally do it but you might find yourself back, particularly if the place where you were was a basic place. And so you'd naturally go back there. I mean, basic in terms of your feelings, your sitting, breathing, your posture, your appreciation of your eyeballs, your appreciation of space in front of you, the wonder of being there again, in the body, sitting, breathing — that's a place you always go back to when you're sitting, or sometimes when you're writing. But then the content — *that* you could never go back to, the freshness of that knowledge.

Do you ever find a few fragments that were separate for a long time, and then you realized that they were connected?

If they were related, I'd put them one, two, three, four. And have done so. Earlier I used to try to tie them together in big formal poems, but it was fakery. And I got more and more interested in just the bare bones of the process as being enough. As being more exemplary, teaching more to other people, and at the same time, teaching me more, and at the same time being more honest. And less weighty, less heavy. Less heavy-handed, less ambitious, less egotistical. And also, you know, there's an awful lot of writing anyway. More writing than anybody can read. You know, the swifter we are at it, the better. You get more chance of being read if you just stick to what you know, rather than trying to construct something you don't know. Though, in the process of constructing something using your spontaneous mind playing, there's also that element of invention and comedy and friendliness that issues forth.

What I'm trying to do is sort of describe the narrow path of practice to get to the mind. How far in the mind we get depends really on the application of practice, the application of meditation, the sincerity of practice, the clarity of the practice as distinct from the ambitiousness of it. The simplicity of the practice as distinct from the greediness of it.

But won't that process continue forever, if you are just writing what your mind is thinking, without any focus of a religious nature? Won't you always be writing about the garbage in your mind?

Well, you're assuming that the mind won't arrive by itself at its own source. That the mind won't want to think about deity or emptiness. I think that most people who try to write spontaneously, write garbage. I'll agree there.

Well, that's what I'm saying, that perhaps there's a need for more self-conscious. . .

Well, you better define what you mean by self-conscious.

Well, having the idiom in mind...

You're saying you have to have a presupposition or precontext. Well, I think that would be contrary to this practice, and I think that until you are accomplished in the practice of observing your own mind, and transcribing it, you can't start off with a prefixed idea. Because then you won't observe your mind, you'll be observing the idea and trying to rationally create an extention of the idea or an image to fit things in. Chogyam Trungpa told me something about two years ago which extended something that Kerouac had also said. Kerouac and· I were worrying about this problem, trying to formu-

late it, and he said that if the mind is shapely, the art will be shapely. Or, "Mind is shapely, art is shapely." It's a question of knowing your mind. So the discipline, in a sense, would be having a mind and knowing it. And then when you're writing, that writing will be interesting according to that actual mind.

But the spontaneity is held in a certain form.

Sometimes. Some spontaneous forms are very formal, like the haiku and the blues. In America, the most extensive practice of spontaneous form is the blues, and calypso, but mostly the blues, and that has a very, very strong form, very definite forms, and that's one of the forms I'd like to teach here — the practical application of blues to Buddhist meditation or something. Anyway, I didn't finish about the other phrase that was a key phrase from 1971 or '72, I guess, here in Boulder. I was writing a spontaneous chain poem with Chogyam and he said, and we finally agreed, "First thought is best thought. That was sort of the formula: first thought, best thought. That is to say, the first thought you had on your mind, the first thought you thought before you thought, yes, you'd have a better thought, before you thought you should have a more formal thought — first thought, best thought. If you stick with first flashes, then you're all right. But the problem is, how do you *get* to that first thought — that's always the problem. The first thought is always the great elevated, cosmic, non-cosmic, *shunyata* thought. And then, at least according to the Buddhist formulation, after that you begin imposing names and forms and all that. So it's a question of catching yourself at your first open thought.

Could you give me an example of spontaneity without form?

Yes, I believe there are examples. I believe Milarepa is an example of spontaneity without form in certain poems. There are certain open poems.

I know, but he was enlightened.

We're all enlightened. Fuck that bullshit enlightenment. There is no enlightenment. If we're going to start waiting to be enlightened to write poetry. . .

EMPTY WORDS

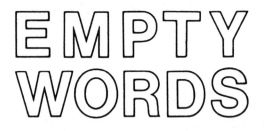

Photo by Bob Del Tredici

JOHN CAGE TALKS BACK

The night Nixon resigned John Cage gave the first performance of *Empty Words—Part IV,* consisting of a mix of vowels, consonants and silences culled by chance operations from the *Journal of Henry David Thoreau.* Slide projections of drawings from the *Journal* slowly appeared and disappeared.

Some of the audience filled in the silences with sounds ranging from guitar playing and bird whistles to catcalls and screams. Through it all John Cage managed a fierce concentration on his piece. When it was over he rose and turned to face his audience. The dialogue follows:

Audience: You've said that the key of sound is that all sounds pertain to nature. And that you are trying to portray that.

Cage: I didn't say that at all. I didn't say I was trying to portray anything — and if you had listened closely you would have understood that.

In light of what happened, do you think you were sucking people out of themselves?

There was no sucking going on. (Uproar). I think we all, I too, not only you, have a good deal of self examination to do. I can tell you a story — it happened years ago, and it has happened throughout my life. This isn't the first time people have tried to make me appear as a fool. I went with Merce Cunningham to Columbus, Ohio, in the forties. We drove night and day through snow and ice, often slipping off the road, to get to Columbus. We arrived so late that there was no time to sleep. We had to prepare in the theatre, and then gave the performance. There was a party afterwards. And at the party everyone told us how miserable our work was, and why did we devote our lives to what we were doing? And I thought at the time, why do we go to such trouble to do these things that people don't enjoy?

Ten years later I received a letter from a person who had been at that particular program, and he thanked me for that performance, and said that it had changed his life. Now whether his life changed for the better we don't know — but at least it gave him some kind of stimulus.

Did you enjoy the noises?

I was doing something I had never done before. And the reason that I decided to do it here was that it occurred to me that it was very beautiful and very appropriate for this circumstance. But then due to my becoming so foolishly famous, many people come to such a performance who have no reason for coming except a foolish curiosity. And when they discover that I'm not nearly so interesting to them as they thought I might be, I don't understand why they don't go away.

Isn't that the chance response you deal with?

I know it, I know what limb I'm out on, I've known it all my life, you don't have to tell me that.

It's just like those slides you showed, the response was just a different thing.

Nonsense. Those slides are by Thoreau and in my opinion they are extremely beautiful. The catcalls and imitations were mere stupid criticisms. The thing that is beautiful about the Thoreau drawings is that they're completely lacking in self-expression. And the thing that made a large part of the public's interruption this evening so ugly was that it was full of self-expression.

Why draw a line?

It's the line that I've drawn, and to which my life is devoted. I had the good fortune in the late forties to go for two years to lectures by Daisetz Suzuki on Zen Buddhism. One of the lectures he gave was on the structure of mind. He drew an oval on the board, and halfway up the left-hand side he put two parallel lines which he said was the ego. "The ego has the capability to close itself in by means of its likes and dislikes. It stays there by day through its sense perceptions and by night through its dreams. What Zen would like, instead of its acting as a barrier, is that the ego would open its doors, and not be controlled by its likes and dislikes."

I want to know how you organized the silent spaces.

When you're dealing, as I was this evening, with just letters and silences, there are three possibilities: one is to have a series of letters, another is to have a series of letters and silences, and the last is to have a series of silences. The *I Ching* works with the number 64. I have made tables for the numbers up to 64. The question is which of the three possibilities are we doing? I assigned to letters alone 1 through 21; 22 through 43 the two together; and 44 through 64 the silences. The whole text this evening began with fourteen seconds of silence, followed by a mixture of letters and silences. I find the letters by asking which of the fourteen volumes I am looking in; which group of pages; which page. Then I count the lines on the page, and then count the letters in the line and find one of the letters. And if there were vowels together, or two or more consonants together, I asked the *I Ching* whether I should take one or more of the consonants or vowels, because in that way one gets diphthongs or other sounds that separate us from the simplicity of the alphabet.

I think the work was a success, I think you really got your point across.

No, I didn't get my point across to you, you got your point across to you. I don't know why you still think people are pushing ideas from one head into another.

Did you end the piece the way you wanted to end it, or did you end it because people were making noise?

I didn't end it the way I wanted to end it, I ended it the way it was to end. Why is it that when I go to hear someone and I don't like what is going on, instead of interrupting it, I say to myself, why don't you like it? Can't you find something about it that you enjoy? People insist upon self-expression. I really am opposed to it. I don't think people should express themselves in that kind of way.

But isn't that what you're doing right now?

I don't think so, I'm discussing this situation, which although you say you enjoyed it, I think could have been a lot more successful.

Haven't you said that you want to incorporate outside noises into your work?

I haven't said that, I've said that contemporary music should be open to the sounds outside it. I just said that the sounds of the traffic entered very beautifully, but the self-expressive sounds of people making foolishness and stupidity and catcalls were not beautiful, and they aren't beautiful in other circumstances either.

But are they a part of the work?

No. They're a part of the experience we have. They are a part of our lives, but are they a part of what we want society to be?

It's what we are.

No — I think society can be different.

Yes, but it's what we can start with, work with.

I must say that since '67 I've worked on the journals of Thoreau. Thoreau said that when he was in the presence of nature, he had a feeling of affirmation about life. He said when he was with people he couldn't find it. I think that answer is easily found without it being told by anyone.

What were your expectations of your performance tonight?

I don't have expectations.

If you're disappointed, then you have expectations.

That goes back to what I said at the beginning, that I felt that it would be beautiful to do this piece in this situation.

Aren't you glad you got an honest response?

If we are talking about the interruptions, that's not to be classified under honest, that's to be classified under the complete absence of self-control and openness to boredom — and boredom comes not from without but from within.

Sadhana and Society

Ram Dass

Most of us have grown up with a preoccupation with individual differences because it's been very efficient, but it's also been very neurotic. We get very discriminating about individual differences, and we call that being sophisticated.

And with our own individual differences we get totally preoccupied. We come through childhood, most of us, with some sense of inferiority, inadequacy, impotence, incompetence. And this sense is emotional and non-conceptual; it's just a feeling that comes from early child-rearing. We don't have to go into the dynamics of how that develops, but it just is a common thing. It is so pervasive that it almost looks like the feelings that would arise out of a sense of original sin, if you want to view it from a religious point of view.

But then we start to identify with our individual differences, with these feelings of inadequacy, or badness, or wrongness, or feelings that we've got to do good in order to be okay. Thus we are working from a basis that we're really kind of rotten, but if we do good things we will be okay.

And usually we find some individual difference in ourself that we can connect with this feeling and thus blame it. I used to be overwhelmed, when I was a psychotherapist, by the fact that each person had his or her 'thing.' And each person said, "If I didn't have a nose that was shaped this way, if my breasts were bigger or smaller, if I were having better orgasms, if I had come from a richer family, if I were a different color, if my parents hadn't broken up when I was young, if I had lived in a neighborhood where I had more kids to play with, if I had had a more compassionate father . . ." Everybody's got their thing. I may not have hit yours exactly, but I hit a good forty percent of us, right?

Now, in the course of sadhana, of spiritual journey, of awakening, of deepening of meditation, our social perceptions keep changing. And many of us are in the peculiar predicament that we have built a whole ego structure about who we are and how we function, based on these tremendously label-laden habits about individual differences. But now we are experiencing realms of the universe that are totally inconsistent with these habits of thought about who we are.

An analogy that is useful to understand these perceptual shifts is the microscope, as though you're focusing through layers of a slide preparation. Because if you look at other people first — the way you traditionally look at them — you look at them, first of all, in terms of your own desire systems. If you're horny you see who's makable, who's a competitor for who's makable, or who's irrelevant. That's your way of dividing the universe. If you're an achiever or power oriented person, you look at who's beatable, or who's going to beat you out. And you see everybody in domains of power. If your preoccupation is color, you see people in terms of color.

Now, if you flip the microscope one little flip, and you look a little deeper into another person, what you begin to see is personality. And then you see everybody as — "That's a cheerful person. That person is very pleasant. That person seems depressed. . ."

O.K., if you flip it once more into another astral plane, you will see astrological things. And then there are only twelve permutations in the world. And you see everybody as Leo or Aries or Sagittarius . . . And when you look at another person, that's what you see. You say, "I'm seeing a Leo." A person says, "I'm not a Leo, my name is Fred." You say, "Well, that's what you *think* you are, but in fact you are a Leo." And that's the reality of that plane.

If you go one more flip, what you see when you look at another person is another person, and he's looking back at you. Right? You look into his eyes and you see somebody else. "Are you in there? I'm here, far out!" And you look at the packaging and you see the packaging. The packaging involves the astral, all the individual differences. There's still somebody separate from you in there, but the individual differences are more like the veils or the packaging of the product. You can say, "Are you in there, I'm in here. Here we are, two beings, two beings."

Now you take a relationship to your mother

or your father or your child, who you've got this long history of treating as that's mother, that's father, that's . . . that's my son, that's my daughter, that's Mary Jane. Hello, little Mary Jane. And then you flip the microscope with Mary Jane and suddenly there's another being inside Mary Jane, who isn't Mary Jane at all. It's not *not* Mary Jane, it's not like it's Sarah Lou, it's just another being saying, "I'm in here too. I'm just like you."

Now it gets very, very far out. For example, in my relation with my father, my father is busy thinking *he is my father*. He knows who he is. He's a Republican, he's a man in his middle seventies, he's somebody who loves his family, he's a good man, he owns this and that, he likes the ball game . . . He knows who he is. The problem is that who that is, is dying, sooner or later. He's already beyond the actuarial age. And not only that, but if he is busy being who he is, and I'm then into the symbiotic role, the complementary role in relation to that, so I'm busy being his son — the limits of our relationship are very two dimensional, they're very flat.

But on the other hand, from where I'm sitting, he's just another being, and it just happened that in this lifetime we took incarnations in which this particular round his karma was that I'm his son (heavy karma), my karma was that he was my father. We are each other's karmic predicament, if you will. But behind it all — you're here? I'm here. Far out! See? Now if I say to him, "Are you here? I'm here," he doesn't know what the hell I'm talking about. "Oh, you're talking that nut talk again." And so my job isn't to come on to him at all. My job isn't to say to him, "Look, you're not my father really." Because he's got a birth certificate and the whole thing. But the point is, that my perception of him is that of another being who is in an incarnation in which he is totally identified with the thoughts that are connected with that incarnation, and he is so deeply identified with them that it is all totally real from how he's looking at it. So we will sit down together and we will talk father and son talk. But all the time I'm doing my mantra and I'm sitting in a place inside myself — which is merely another plane, it's no better or worse than the one he's on. It's just a different one in which we are two beings who are doing this dance together.

The point is that no matter what your relationship is with whom, the same rules apply. It doesn't matter if it's your parents, or your child,

Brushwork by Eugene Gregan

Neem Karoli Baba

or your enemy, or your friend, or your therapy patient, or your therapist. You treat them all the same way. You treat them with compassion, you treat them with an appreciation of the fact that we are beings who are incarnations. You quiet yourself, you center yourself. And then it's all possible. And in every relationship it's all possible. Because you're not laying trips on everybody around you all the time. Because you're not sitting around judging — "You should be this way. If you were a good father, you'd be . . ., my child is gonna be . . ., I'm hoping for my therapy patients, that they will . . ., I expected more from a therapist than . . " Can you hear all those places? "I expect my husband to . . ."

See, the predicament is that everybody is doing just what they can do. Maharaji kept saying to me, "Ram Dass, don't you see it's all perfect?" Everybody's just being. When you go out into the woods and you see all the trees you don't say, "Well, that tree isn't like that tree, I wish it were . ., if that tree didn't bend like that it would be a good tree." Somehow with trees you can allow it, you can allow that each tree is just perfect the way it is. But when you get to people, if everybody isn't just how you think they ought to be, all hell breaks loose. So the trick is to look at someone who's hung up and tight and angry and insecure and anxious and frightened, and see the perfection of it. Far out! And you give each incarnation space to manifest as it needs to manifest. You know, five years ago I was busy trying to change my father. And now I have grown enough so I can leave him alone. I can just love him as he is.

The predicament we have with human relationships is recognizing that certain relationships have been laid on us by God, karmically, for this entire incarnation. You don't trade in your father. You don't trade in your child, although you may try. Whether or not you trade in your husband or wife is an interesting issue in this culture at this moment. But at the moment there are certain contractual relationships you're involved in, in which there are things given you're not going to get out of in this lifetime, and there are others that when you get finished with them you can walk away and form new ones. But if you try to walk away from one prematurely, if you can look back with an astral eye, you will see these long threads going to these beings. Like somebody who splits from home and—"Screw you, I'm leaving." Maybe the work was done, but maybe it wasn't. There's a subtle flow of emotions that suggests that it wasn't quite all done. "I'm leaving you and I'm taking the children. I've finished my work with you!" You may go away for a while, but that's okay. Later on you'll be cooler, you'll understand. You can't go through the door as long as you leave unfulfilled karmic stuff behind you. Now sometimes you've walked away from somebody, and then they died. You say, "Oh, I've blown it." Not necessarily. When you get totally centered, you can run through the relationship with them and bring it up to date consciously — life and death isn't what it's about.

I remember a dialogue I had with Trungpa. He said to me, "Ram Dass, what do you do about sorcerers?" And I said, "What sorcerers, I don't see any sorcerers." And he said, "Don't cop out, what do you do about sorcerers?" I said, "Trungpa, I don't notice all that stuff. I just notice God, it's all One, it's none of my business. I'm just aiming for the One." Now he and I have been having a continuous dialogue, which is a very interesting one about responsibility. And if I deny the sorcerers and deny this physical plane

with evil and good, deny the individual differences, I am caught in denial for fear of all this stuff. Then I am no less hung up than if I had been totally preoccupied with individual differences, and failed to appreciate that behind it all lies the One. And what my growth is, is that I am growing able to assume the responsibility in the realm of individual differences, at the same moment keeping fully aware that One lies behind it all. Like people say to me, "Oh thank you, you're so wonderful. And you've done so much for my life." I say, "I don't do anything, I'm just a pawn in the game." And they say, "Oh come on, stop kidding me." Now from where I'm sitting, that's the most real thing I can say. At another level it is true that I am doing something or other. And if I deny one level and cling to another, I'm still caught. So when people thank me, I say, "You're welcome." And when they say, "You didn't do it," I say, "You're right." And you learn to live with such paradoxes.

Within the Romantic image is the word *loneliness*. A lot of people feel very lonely when they get into certain psychological spaces where they don't make contact with others. Loneliness is part of the melodrama. You're alone and everybody's left you, and you're in your room and nobody cares, you're unloved, and you're full of self pity. And you're sitting there and you're lonely. And to the extent that you have any centering or meditative position left, there is that little cosmic humor voice in you that says, "Boy is this terrible, am I . . . Oh, look at this self pity. You could cut it with a knife . . . Am I lonely." And there is a connoisseur in you that is appreciating the essence of loneliness, the kind of intense quality of the suffering. And as you sit quieter with that or with any of your emotional states, you begin to experience a peace right in the midst of the melodrama. And that peace is a peace in which you feel totally quiet. It is not a social sense.

It turns out that what we are all starting to experience is *satsang*, or a community of the spirit, or a community of consciousness, that is not in time and space. But we are so habituated to thinking of relationships with people in time and space that we keep running through old dramas even though we've used them up. So that you get the experience where somebody goes away from you and you say, "Oh, I'll miss you," and you go through a whole melodrama of "Goodbye, I'll miss you, it's horrible you're leaving," and yet a few minutes later you're fully involved with what you're doing right then, and you don't miss them at all. And when you see them again it seems like only a moment.

Do you think that if our bodies — these big, grotesque, decaying bodies — get together and we hug and we do a thing, it'll somehow be more than it was before? Now it's not at the level of knowing, it's at the level of being that I say to people, "There is nobody that I could ever miss again." Because nobody could ever get away from me again. Nor I from them. Because I don't live on a physical time-space plane. And when you start to live not on the physical time-space plane, you realize that our coming and going isn't what it's about. When you realize that our coming and going is not what it's about, you could never be lonely again. You couldn't possibly be lonely, because — where could you go? I mean, how can I get away from my guru? Do you think if I go in my bathroom and lock the door I can be lonely? I can't be. It's always one thought away. The living spirit, the community of our consciousness, that Guru inside, is always one thought away.

When you're busy being lonely all you have to do is sit down and meditate. Because one thought away, the minute you give up the thought of yourself as separate, which is the one that's lonely — here we are again. Here we are again. And when you are in the *here we are again* there is a place where you have turned your microscope where there's another being and another being and another being just like you, but if you turn it once more there is only *one of it*. And that is the great aloneness. That is the place that comes through very, very deep meditative space, the experience of the fact that all forms and all separateness is just a passing show, it's just stuff. And there really is only — Aaahhhhh — that's the aloneness. And when you live in that, you know that even though you'll meet many people, you will always be alone. Not lonely, but always alone. Not separate, but always alone.

It is not a bad meditation to sit down and meditate on your own divinity, on your own beauty. Just to start to dislodge, force to the surface, all that negative stuff you've got about who you think you are. There was a time a few years ago, in 1964 or '65, I went to California and I thought, "Gee, you know, I've done an awful lot of rotten things in my life, do you suppose I'm evil? Do you suppose there's like something just basically corrupt and rotten in me?" So I kept working with this problem, "Do you suppose I'm evil? Gee, I must be. I guess I am really evil." And then in February of that year I took a very deep acid trip by myself. And I went in and in, and I went to where I really felt evil. I stood in front of a mirror and I became as evil as I could. And I went through all my evil thoughts. I was really scaring the hell out of myself — literally. And then I went back and back and back and I came to a place in me where I just am. I do a lot of crummy things and I do a lot of beautiful things. And I am neither good nor evil, I just am. There's good, there's evil, and I am.

That experience was incredibly suffery, there was a lot of genuine suffering in that whole business. But that suffering was such incredible grace in terms of my own evolution. And if I can keep reiterating to you that the quicker you can get the perception where you understand that suffering is grace, the more you're going to have *all of it* become the teaching, all of it. And you won't just become preoccupied with self pity. And as you purify, and as you meditate more deeply, you become a more pure seeker, and that purity of seeking makes you keep seeing through the illusion over and over and over again.

The work with each other is that work. The work is — not getting lost in individual differences. Honor them, recognize them, honor them in yourself, work with them. Keep looking behind, through your love of truth, or your love of the One, or your love of reality, until every relationship becomes more of a teaching. Because until you are free, the only work you have to do is work on yourself. And everything you do with everybody becomes a vehicle for that work on yourself.

LIFE
IN THE BRUSH

Richard Greene

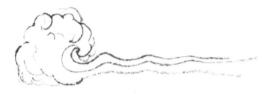

consider materials and colors carefully, and then slowly proceed to the study of rocks, of trees, of living things. All training evolves as a continual reference to a set body of knowledge: Six Canons, Six Essentials, Six Qualities, Three Faults, and Twelve Things to Avoid. The student gains confidence and ease as he becomes familiar enough with the tradition to imitate the masters. As with many classical arts, absolute mastery of technique precedes individual expression. One doesn't enter hurriedly; the Chinese approached it with a calmness typical of a culture grounded in spiritual disciplines.

When Eugene Gregan met his brush painting class at Naropa Institute this summer, the context was quite different. The course lasted only five weeks. Students came from eclectic backgrounds; their skills varied greatly. A few were artists experienced in other media; many were novices fascinated by a late entry in the Naropa course listings, *Life in the Brush*. Although many were in some way familiar with Buddhism, no one was versed in Chinese culture or the practice of the Tao. We were generally quite young, clearly lacking the maturity of accomplished Chinese statesmen/artists. Gene Gregan is hardly a model of a Chinese master painter, being young, American and non-monastic in orientation, with extensive training and experience in the fine arts, but not in Buddhism or Taoism. I wondered how we could even approach experiencing whatever it is the Chinese do in their painting.

Brush painting is an old and integral part of Chinese culture. The great masters have seldom been strict "artists" in the Western sense, but have come to painting as an expression of maturity, after significant accomplishments in politics, music, poetry, scholarship, astronomy or other traditional arts. Only after understanding and practicing the Tao did the Chinese turn to painting as an "extension of the art of living."

Brush painting reaffirms the tradition of the Tao, transmitting the principles and methods developed by earlier masters. The beginner needs a solid understanding of Chinese ideographs and the art of calligraphy and must be willing to undertake years of preparation to develop skills and master the traditional forms of symbolic representation. The classic Chinese text on the subject, *The Mustard Seed Manual*, stresses hard work. "Take ten days to paint a stream and five to paint a rock, study ten thousand volumes and walk ten thousand miles." The student is urged to begin with one school of painting and master its brushstroke techniques, to

But the instructor reflected the sincerest optimism about initiating Americans into the process of brush painting. He was delighted with students who had come for what he considered to be the best of reasons—they wanted to paint. No one had been assigned the course, it wasn't required. The Naropa context had no overtly ambitious and acquisitive element and presented the possibility of detached work and sincere exploration.

The drawing began with a stilling process which enabled us to forget what we thought we knew (or didn't know) about painting. For the novice, it meant dealing with the overwhelming tendency to decry inexperience and incompetence and thus avoid taking a plunge. For artists, perhaps the more difficult task of letting go of well-learned opinions, approaches, and even technical skills.

As a meditation, we began each session with the grinding of our daily ink supply on inkstones; we tried to get a tactile feel for the medium, to slow down, and to involve ourselves deliberately with the *process* of brush painting. Sometimes we took as an object of meditation a tree or landscape, which allowed us to become familiar with the visual image

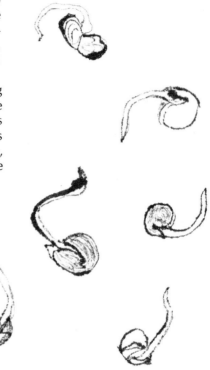

we were dealing with. As in the *Mustard Seed Manual,* "He who is learning to paint must first still his heart, thus to clarify his understanding and increase his wisdom."

Our first assignments evolved from the use of a very fine number zero or double-zero red sable brush. We started with a sharp focus, creating a microscopic impression of the organic world. We spent almost two weeks studying the detailed patterns of veins in leaves, the symmetrical bud-structures of stems, the swirls in pine cones, and fine hairs on blades of grass. At home we sprouted seeds and drew the changing forms of garbanzo beans, avocados, and alfalfa sprouts.

Each day our evolution, like the plants', was recorded in the diaries we were urged to keep. Gene asked us to always be aware of the kind of drawings we made, and the best way was to keep a record of what had come earlier: nothing was to be discarded. The evolutionary process seemed to dominate Gene's approach in the technique of drawing organisms as well. With organic sequence as our guide, we learned to draw stems before leaves, veins before petals, petals before flowers; we drew from the inside out, just as a seed grows, unfolds. The "seed idea" enabled us to deal with structure, grounded in the spontaneous way the world evolves.

We were forced to deal with the extreme complexity of living organisms. Devoting an hour to a pine cone teaches not only a lot about conifers, but suggests that the artist must re-examine complexity and detail if he or she is to deal with the scale of landscape painting. And so we began to change the focus and learned to represent the same substances with less detail and more stylization. One three-part assignment involved going to nearby Boulder Creek to first draw a rock in the stream, then draw water in the stream, and finally from what we'd learned in the first two drawings,

show a rock in the water. We'd jumped a level; we were no longer strictly copying what was before us. Now we had to deal with not only the visual images, but also with how we might simplify and symbolize them, capturing the essence of movement and life in "rocks and water." It was quite a new experience to try to draw something like water that wouldn't wait for us—stand still for us. This forced us to *feel* more deeply, beyond surface structure and design, to understand the essential rhythms underlying all natural forms. We collected symbols based on our feel for the visual world around us. This was the beginning of our vocabulary.

No sooner had we begun a progression from micro-focus to the collection of symbols when Gene asked us to purchase a large, wide ink brush. Our problem had changed: we stood in class over our drawing tables, full hand over the brush, with nothing to draw from, no mountains, no flower arrangement, no clouds. We were told to draw a large, bold circle on the paper and, while the brush was still in motion, to drop to the center and there represent a living form, a symbol. The paintings required no longer than a minute, the style reminded me of Oriental calligraphy: some aspect of the form is simply represented while the overall impact is at once stylized and personal.

The graphic circle was used by ancient Hindus to represent the idea of zero or, in Sanskrit, *shunya,* from which eventually Buddhism developed the tradition of experiencing *shunyata* or voidness. Gene's classroom problem urged us to relate to this idea of "the undefined." After weeks of concrete detailing and symbolizing, dropping "into the void" came as quite a shock. I wanted a model; I had an absolutely certain feeling that I "didn't know what to draw." There was no grounding, no security, and no way to know what would happen after the circle closed.

The first drawings were hesitant, but Gene encouraged us relentlessly. "Don't stop, don't wait, don't look back. Push yourself a little, and be deliberate." It seemed paradoxical to be deliberate in a painting that was finished as soon as it was begun. But there wasn't much to lose, and after twenty or thirty drawings and a lot of ink grinding, we

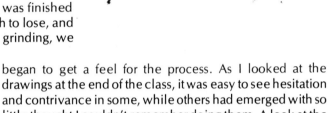

began to get a feel for the process. As I looked at the drawings at the end of the class, it was easy to see hesitation and contrivance in some, while others had emerged with so little thought I couldn't remember doing them. A look at the class's work showed we did have "something in mind" and in a surprising way we knew what we were doing. Perhaps our best work came from this exercise; we had been pushed from our safe position and we saw the creative possibilities in jumping quickly and deliberately into new territory.

The outcome of an undertaking is never what we imagine it to be beforehand. I went into the course hoping simply to study painting, but found that I did so decidedly in the context of spiritual thought and practice. And inasmuch as that particular artistic tradition is an embodiment of a cultural/spiritual tradition, there seems to be no way to have one without the other.

Brushwork by Greg Coffey, Patricia Daniels, Seth Levinson, Rick Merrill, and Cathy Zimmerman.

EMBODIMENT

A discussion with
Deborah Katz
Ben Weaver
Arlyn Ray
Judyth Weaver

in Dance, T'ai Ch'i Ch'uan,

and Sensory Awareness

D. Campbell: Deborah, what brought you here? What have you been doing here?

D. Katz: I'm teaching a course called Dance and Meditation, which tries to bridge the gap between body and mind. People have a sense that they want to dance, and they have a feeling that they have been trapped. The Dance Meditation class is hopefully cutting through that. Dancing seems to be a response to an impulse — there seems to be a necessity to understand what our relationship is with the body: What is the body? Who are we? Who am I? That's the essence of what I'm working with in Dance and Meditation.

B. Weaver: I'm teaching sensory awareness, which also approaches this question of body and mind. Our way of doing it is to try to get underneath the concepts that tend to filter and condition our experience, to come to a direct experience of ourselves in the *Now*. Instead of working with dance forms or particular kinds of movement, we do experiments. We work with stones. We work with simple things like sitting, walking, lying, and standing. We roll down hills. We get in touch with gravity. It is all at the kindergarden level, but it is also very powerful and effecting. People go through some extraordinary changes, just really experiencing themselves at this elemental level.

A. Ray: I teach Indian classical dance, which is very different from the courses just described. It is based on structure, form, and discipline. It is very much an art of Asia, highly devotional and spiritual, in a very set way. Everything about the dance is already defined. The dancers are working with prescribed movements, and their own emotions, and their relationship to the story, myth or concept behind the dance.

J. Weaver: I'm teaching T'ai Ch'i Ch'uan, a form of movement meditation. It is a very traditional form which as you practice it, and perform it, brings you to a point of formlessness. The movements are very prescribed and in performing them day after day repetitively, you come to a point beyond, which is a meditation. You come to an awareness of your bodily structure, how you relate to gravity and the world. Eventually, in longer range, it becomes a form of self defense, but we're not emphasizing that.

D. Campbell: One of the premises of Naropa Institute has been to focus on the interrelationship between intellect and intuition. I wonder to what degree the preconceived split we seem to have between body and mind is reflected in that notion. It seems that people are seeking to get more in touch with their bodies as a way of making their entire experience more complete, concentrating on the larger intelligence which is more than just developing the intellect, as is the case in most university structures. I wonder what you feel has evoked this interest?

B. Weaver: I'm very glad that Rinpoche and the faculty invited me to teach sensory awareness here. Many people came to my classes and said, "Sensory awareness seems to be a good balance for me, for the intellectual things I'm taking in other courses." I was astonished to see how many people were interested. I've been teaching at growth centers for about five years, and I've never had such large groups. Now suddenly, a lot of people are interested in my work, interested in T'ai Ch'i, in dance, in meditation, interested in such a demanding discipline as Indian classical dance. There is a great interest by the students in balance and harmony. I'm delighted by what the students have brought to Naropa.

D. Katz: I think there is a very interesting thing happening here about the idea of intellect and body. There are some very "intellectual" classes and there are some "experiential" classes. But what I think is happening is that all the intellectual classes are forcing the students to realize that there is no intellectual "thing." The intellectual is actually experiential; when it gets right down to it, there actually is no difference. There still seems to be this split, with people talking "intellectual" and "experiential"; but in the intellectual realm there is a realization that there is no way out, one can't mouth things anymore. There is this feeling of fruitlessness, of hopelessness, about just stating theories or ideas. People just can't stand that gap anymore — where people are sitting around in a room talking about ideas instead of *being* what they are talking about.

D. Campbell: People still seem to feel that the body and mind are not entirely related, and that if one has body problems, one does a body discipline, and if one wants greater clarity, one does an intellectual discipline. You're suggesting that mind and body are one continuous organism, that they are not separate . . . ?

D. Katz: I think so. Not only do I *think* so, but on occasion I *know* so. It has been interesting having studied dance for twenty years, having learned, absolutely in terms of my body how to do this motion, this movement — and then finding out after twenty years that I couldn't dance. I had been learning the motions, but I didn't know how to dance. So then there was the question, "What is dancing? What is going on here? Who am I?" It always came back to "Who am I? Am I my body? Who is pushing this body around?" There was this great confusion. Probably people who haven't had such an extreme bodily discipline can get away with a more experiential relationship with their body — but the split was so great between my body and my mind that I was forced to reconcile it.

A. Ray: Do you think it is possible that out of discipline can come a kind of freedom? You can learn a technique, you can learn how to do something thoroughly and then you can be creative, then you can open up to the experience.

D. Katz: Absolutely . . .

J. Weaver: If it is a full discipline. Our western dilemma is mind over body, where we have brought our mind under control, and use our body as nothing more than a machine. There's no freedom there . . .

D. Katz: I saw a film called *Phantom India,* by Louis Malle. In one section he showed a dance school in South India, started by Annie Besant. It was of these girls and boys learning how to dance, and I realized that these people were learning how to use their emotions in their dance. Their emotions existed just as any other part of them, and they were dealt with in that proper way. You have hurt, fear, happiness, gladness, sadness, or love, and not just their shells; these emotions can be used . . . We seem to be victims of our emotions in the West . . .

B. Weaver: There are other things contributing here, too. Our common language . . . I hear people saying, "I'm going to take the 'bod' home and put it in a tub." There is this tremendous distance between who we really are . . . We are alive, these are our feelings, our vitality; and yet there is this cool distance that we've set up in the way that we think and talk about this so-called mind. Yet underneath that we have a primitive experience of unity, of being a whole organism . . .

D. Campbell: Where do you think this disrespect for the body comes from? It seems that in America even things like "body building" are another form of disrespect for the body, not accepting your body as who you are . . .

B. Weaver: Well, we are very hung up on mastery and control in this culture.

D. Katz: What is peculiar is that it is through this sort of objectification of the body . . . we have this thing that as soon as we are born, somehow our bodies are sinful. It seems to come from the Christian tradition.

D. Campbell: But do you think that's unique to the West? In some yogic practices in the East isn't there some desire to escape the body?

A. Ray: Yes, there is, in some oriental traditions.

D. Campbell: Where do you think this comes from — this desire to escape the body as if it were not an adequate home for the spirit . . . that there is something impoverished about it?

A. Ray: I think it starts way back when we are children, and not being honored. It's not being honored as beings. Not just bodies, not just minds, but as beings. If you are allowed to grow up with the full sense of being that every child starts out with, and not being squished one way or the other, then you grow up with a sense of yourself. And it comes from other things too, like sitting in chairs that don't fit us, wearing clothes that make us uncomfortable, so we are not honoring ourselves in those non-verbal ways . . .

B. Weaver: What we have been hitting at here

is the whole question of "image." We are pre-eminently people of the image. Nobody cares what it is like on the inside, if it looks good, is proper on the outside. People come to my classes and they think they have a good sense of who they are — they have a whole pastiche of images. The classes break those down — we try to bring people to an experience of themselves within . . . It is so revolutionary, to feel "Gee, it's all right to see how I am from the inside, rather than try to put on another image."

A. Ray: And the images aren't just put on in the West, I have a feeling that the images exist universally. That's what spirituality is all about — getting in touch with something not just beyond your body, but getting in touch with your body *and* mind . . .

D. Campbell: I think people sometimes associate "spirituality" with transcending the body, getting some special higher consciousness that doesn't have anything to do with the body. What you seem to be saying is that "spirituality" is a way of getting a sense of your own basic being . . .

A. Ray: I think that is very much the case. And not just your own body, but other people, because we don't live alone, isolated in the world. We are constantly interacting with everything around us, with nature. And that is what spirituality is, I believe.

D. Katz: And it is a very real thing, it is like having to pay attention to what is going on . . .

A. Ray: Exactly. It's being present.

D. Campbell: And your body's the vehicle for that — the constant reminder, with its insecurities, its problems, its dilemmas. All the irritations, all the restlessness is another way of being aware, of being present.

D. Katz: And that's what people discovered when they were taking acid — looking in mirrors and seeing that they were changing every minute. So that the body really is a manifestation of the mind. I think part of the problem is that we die — you know that ultimately you are going to lose your body. The idea of impermanence comes in, nothing is here forever.

D. Campbell: It seems then that what we are really talking about is a way of coming to accept the body rather than working on it to improve it, transcend it, or escape it.

D. Katz: But the idea of a discipline is a valid thing . . .

D. Campbell: Yes, Arlyn was mentioning that without some kind or form of discipline, whether it be meditation, or T'ai Ch'i Ch'uan, or dance,

there's no reference point, there's no place to begin learning about body/mind. If one attempts to *be* in some formless way it becomes sloppy, neurotic, even lazy. Maybe we don't agree on that . . .

B. Weaver: Well, I've met some highly developed beings who've had no forms besides what they did in their daily life. People living in backwoods log cabins, carving wood. You look at their house, you look at the way they live . . . very, very highly developed beings . .

J. Weaver: That's their form. Our basic form is our everyday life. Whatever we bring in to enhance it, because you might be a certain kind of person and you are attracted to other kinds of things or just want to learn them, is another form. Our basic form is getting up in the morning, and standing up, and doing what you are doing . . .

D. Campbell: Achieving a sort of simple existence which is in tune with nature may be possible for some people, but for the great majority of people, it is not possible. That's not the way society is. There is, for most of us, a life situation which is not the ideal. Can people work with that life situation without completely remaking it into some other style?

J. Weaver: Very definitely. You don't have to move to the country, you don't have to do anything. My Zen master in Japan once said to me, "Sure it's easy living here in the monastery, but when you're down in the middle of town, and when the bus honks its horn, can you achieve enlightenment then?" That's where it is. It doesn't matter where you are, it matters how you are. It doesn't matter what you do, it's how you do it. You can become just as aware of everything in the middle of New York City as you can on a mountain top. It's your awareness and sense, and you can do it anywhere. Most people who achieved enlightenment didn't do it sitting on a meditation cushion, but in stumbling across a stone or something, as they were on their way to somewhere . . .

D. Katz: It seems that what meditation is, is simply being where one is, in the moment. In terms of teaching, to realize *what is* teaching, in dancing, to realize *what is* dancing — reconciling oneself with what is going on, seeing what is happening. Respecting exactly where one is.

D. Campbell: Accepting it . . .

A. Ray: Totally.

D. Katz: Accepting it. Then one can really do anything. One can dance, read a book, be a teacher, be a student — really *anything*!

Metaknowledge
and the Logic of Buddhist Language

Ives Waldo

Gregory Bateson suggests that there is an affinity between some of his work with learning and logical types and Mahayana philosophy as represented by Zen.[1] Until now the matter has gone no further, perhaps because not many people are interested in both contexts. As it happens, it is a very fruitful suggestion. Many statements are quite clear in the light of the theory of types that cannot be expressed unparadoxically without it. Buddhist concepts like shunyata (emptiness), anatman (egolessness), and the two truths distinction are of this sort. They can only be straightforwardly elucidated in terms of a hierarchical structure of viewpoints. The attempt to collapse them into a single type yields nonsense. It is this that causes people to say that Buddhist thought cannot be dealt with logically, or by "linear logic." But the approach we are concerned with is not in that sense a linear logic.

Bateson divides learning phenomena into (at least) four levels, each of which is "about" the level below.

Level 0: This involves recognition and re-recognition of stimuli leading to a repertory of responses that are basically fixed, "wired-in" in the sense of being innate and unchangeable. It is a collapsed sense of learning as "knowledge" of stimuli that are significant in terms of a behavioral repertory.

Level 1: This is learning about Level 0, involving change of stimulus-response connections. It includes the familiar Pavlovian and instrumental learning contexts of experimental psychology.

Level 2: This is learning about contexts of Level 1. The simplest case is that of "learning to learn" in experimental animals. E.g., rats that have run mazes before learn new mazes more quickly than those without such experience. Experienced rote learners do better than those unfamiliar with this sort of learning *context.*

Veteran Skinner rats have an idea that responses like button pushing are relevant in a laboratory context.

A bit more complex are Lashley's rats who know mazes blindfolded, swim through them when flooded, roll with tied feet, etc. Simple stimulus-response links cannot explain such conditioning. On a hierarchic model — perhaps involving stochastic behavior in terms of sub-goals, the sort of thing chess-playing computers do — there is hope of accounting for such behavior.

It is worth noting that with this sort of structure one can model in switching-circuits behavior that we feel inclined to describe with words like "purpose," "choice," "exploration," etc. What seems like anthropomorphizing with "ghosts in machines" on one level becomes on this model a structure capable of absolutely precise mathematical specification.

Bateson sees this level as concerned with one's style of behavior, one's character as a more or less thematically unified set of dispositional motifs *about* behavior. Such styles might be individual or cultural. They differ from Ryle's notions of mental acts as behavioral dispositions by being dispositions of such dispositions. From the repertory of habitual responses directed at some end or expression, one chooses those that tally with some overriding notion of what one is — some things fit the style, others do not. This includes one's conceptual style too, usually in terms of membership in a cultural climate of opinion — scientific, religious, magical, or whatever. It is a world-view and a form of life at once.

Knowledge on this level, being largely attitudinal, is in no direct way verifiable or falsifiable. For this reason reconditioning one's basic character, cultural outlook, or religious viewpoint is notoriously difficult. It also tends to be minimally conscious, unexamined in a Socratic sense. People tend to take culturally received or imprinted viewpoints of how things are and of their own nature as absolutes, the only way things could be. They expect total correlation of reality with their projectional models.

Level 3: This is knowing in which one becomes conscious of the range of possibilities that exist on Level 2. Now conscious evolution of Level 2 responses in terms of a goal specifiying which sorts of such responses are to be desired becomes possible. Here there is no presupposition that any particular world view or behavioral-emotional pattern of the Level 2 type is an ultimate. One examines without dwelling, uses whatever seems appropriate to the situation, and continually evolves more adequate modes. Thus terms like "dialectic," "evolution," and "creative" come into their own on this level. One has moved from problem solving to inventing new contexts that suggest a whole new array of problems. We have here something analogous to Kuhn's distinction of everyday science and revolutionary science. Revolutionary science involves developing a whole new methodology and paradigm structure of what is involved in doing science.[2]

Bateson suggests that the attempts to change one's character involved in psychoanalysis and in disciplines like Buddhism operate at this level. This suggests both a cognitive interpretation and a psychological function for statements like "there is no ego," "nothing exists," and the like.

Let us first examine the structure of the anatman concept. Hinayana thought, as the term is used in Tibet, is mostly on Level 2. There is a world of dharmas, and a right way to look at them. Anatta means that there is no self over and above a relational resultant of these dharmas. Ego seems to be something solid and controllable that can work its projects on the world, but meditation reveals that ego is not "ours" at all. It is a structure, script, game, or whatever, determined by genetics, society, and family structure for the most part. Moreover, it is neither particularly unified in terms of a cognitive/emotional pattern, nor is it something from which we can stand back with some independent rational part and make judgements. There is no such solid core anywhere to be found. Things then seem rather hopeless. One sees that there is something compulsive, arbitrary, and insane about one's scripts and projects, but one *is* them, so what to do?

At this point one takes refuge in the Dharma hoping that it will allow the building of a sort of alternative Level 2 structure that will not be hopeless. One finds in meditation that there is a sense of space when one seems to be "outside" the problem for short periods — perhaps there would be a state where this was constant, and the ego game would become extinct.

This is really problematical — one is reminded of Dostoyevski's statement that the religious ideal of the good man would have to be some sort of idiocy. But it would also be something of a disaster to proceed to the next stage without certain insights from this level:

1. The ego script is arbitrary.
2. The ego script is inescapable by any effort of one's own.
3. The game of ego cannot be won.

Hinayana emphasis on suffering and transiency makes it clear that the approach of greater skill at ego games is not the answer. Without this base, the chances are that Level 3 ideas would appear simply as means to manipulate people.

At a certain point, as Level 3 openness begins to dawn within Level 2, one realizes that one's character and its total matrix is quite arbitrary — the result of a sort of hypnosis. There is also a potentiality for a vast range of responses to various human situations. This can be quite intoxicating. There is nothing impermissible. A certain actor's mentality develops. One's responses to situations can be worked up and manipulated, and one finds that it's possible to get people to do all sorts of things in this way. Why not be whatever is convenient? Sincerity seems both senseless and impossible. The cynical watcher is a soldier of fortune, a lady of situations, someone Byronically alienated and romantic. Laing has described how such dissociation carried to an extreme makes the world ever flatter and more tinselly, the watcher ever more solid and powerful, until one becomes quite schizophrenic.

One is here trying to model Level 3 on Level 2 and it won't work. It seems at first that some Olympian god-like self ought to control all these possibilities and manifestations. What Hinayana contributes here is a realization that this fantasy of control is hopeless. The responses and manipulatory desires are no more under one's control than the original character. It's quite irrational, and the watcher doesn't *do* anything at all, except distance the emotions into something dreamlike. The romantic still has some pretty definite ideas about what ought to be going on, and this results in an unacceptable reality with alienated and fairytale overtones.

Level 3 proper seems to involve the fading of this structure. There is a growing sense of the continuity of the self-pole of one's situation with the social and environmental setting. In the cynical stage one is embattled, one's territory pushed back until most of the mind is held by "them," continually raped and mortgaged out by the alien forces, except for the little speck of the watcher, which becomes a very quick and clever, but desperate, hunted animal. Level 3 opens this hell into vastly greater space. There is a polarity of self and other, but not a barrier as such.

One has shifted from emphasis on playing one's role to having become a dramatist and stylist in one's own right. There is a delight in working with the rich possibilities of communication with others, but of course this is not something separate from one's own activity — there is no separation into giving, giver, gift, and recipient, as they say in classical terms.

Within Level 2, non-identity with ego as the subject-pole of situations is indistinguishable from total loss of structure and control, or its purposeful destruction. But superimposing another logical level does not eliminate the old organization — it makes it possible to relate to it more inclusively, not identifying with it and excluding everything else. In Level 3 it is evident that the currents constituting the existence and action of the Level 2 personality go all over the map. It then becomes possible to work with them in an intelligent, ecological fashion.

Shunyata is an extension of anatman. Really it is the same thing, once it is realized that one's whole sense of cultural drama and world-view are as much a part of ego-structure as the roles with which one formerly identified. The setting is seen to be an aspect of the drama, and not something absolute given prior to its development. To open oneself to the differences of other people from our preconceptions is also to open oneself to the non-absoluteness of any particular world-view. One's ways of conceptual organization do not vanish, which like losing one's character structure would result in complete helplessness. But their significance and context are viewed differently.

Let us consider the idea of science as an analogy. In the late nineteenth century there was a tendency to identify science with the then current content and method in the belief that it was an essentially finished structure. Today we are all Shunyavadins about science. We rather expect periodic revolutionary advances that will radically change the content and methodological paradigms of science. Our notion of science stands for something one logical type higher than the present state of the art. There is no concrete way of describing *what* it stands for, since on this level science describes an open-ended relationship between such "whats." One describes it by showing how science has developed until now, and then writes "etc." for one knows not what. In Buddhism every way we have of organizing and dealing with situations is seen as relative and open-ended in this way.

At the beginning it can be frightening to get a sense that all one's ideas about what there is are arbitrary. The forced realization that persons and situations are not at all what one thought can give rise to a tremendous sense of inadequacy. One feels trapped in the world of one's projections, others being a world to themselves, and reality being impossible to pin down. There is a constant banging about in the dark, trying to make one's models conform closely enough to what there is so that embarrassing collisions aren't always occurring. Then occasionally there is the sense that one really does understand a little of what someone else is like. It seems either totally irrelevant or quite incompatible with one's own structure — in any case something entirely alien that gives rise to an extremely uncomfortable sensation that one's whole world might momentarily fall apart.

It gradually begins to emerge that the pictures of the "real world" we are making guesses about and the "real" others we wish to contact have no more absolute status than that of the Level 2 ego. They are simply its stage set. If "I" am nothing apart from relations to my human and physical environment, and only emerge as something significant in such relations, the same must be true for others. They and the environment come into significant existence for us only in terms of what can be done in interaction with them. Shunyata arises from realizing the identity of reality, significance, and such interactional situations. To say that situations are empty of ultimate reality is to say there is no sense in looking for a pre-interactional reality. Elements cannot be specified independently of their contexts. So there cannot be a primal stratum of reality, knowable independently of all else, from which all other sorts of meaningfulness are constructed (this is what the concept of dharma elements of the *Sarvastivadins* and others was meant to do). We cannot say for sure what the limits of our possibilities are. We are an ongoing evolutionary (not necessarily progressive) process of creation of the world as significant structure.

Many tortuously convoluted statements in Buddhism are attempts to make such Level 3 statements as we have made above in Level 2 philosophical terms. Thus we find Nagarjuna claiming that there is no self, then that there neither is nor is not, then that there is, but that being not separate from other things it has no absolute nature, and finally that there is no way of saying what he wants to say. Exactly similar prevarications surround the attempt to define shunyata. Things neither exist nor do not exist, and this is identical with the fact that all things arise interdependently. From this arises in a direct line the *koan* style of Rinzai, the very apotheosis of Buddhist irrationality.

Yet it seems that some of the "unspeakable truths" of Buddhism have been stated above. Their form is no more complex than distinguishing language and reality, realizing that this sentence is not written on "paper," and the like. We can then see the relation of these ideas to western ideas, which I think is a necessary prelude to taking Buddhism seriously as an intellectual force. From the little we have done here it should be evident that Buddhism, with twenty-five hundred years of experience in psychological engineering, has a great deal to contribute to the social sciences, whose conceptions and methods are still very much in tentative stages of development.

There is a possible objection to this arising from the traditional place of paradox in the teaching methods of the Buddhist path. Buddhism is concerned not only with intellect but with all the deeply rooted habits of emotion, perception, and action that constitute the significance of our world. Bateson points out that the higher the logical type of some bit of conditioning, the more remote its connection to experience and the harder it is to work with. Level 2 changes are difficult (changing character or world view) and production or modification at Level 3 (involved in enlightenment) is a Herculean endeavor.

Paradox has traditionally played a part here. We can compare what happens in the process of a scientific revolution. Scientists persist with traditional methods until every possible avenue of escape is shown to be inadequate. Then they become open to change, and a period of hunting ensues until a new approach emerges. Similarly a traditional prelude to awareness in Buddhism is the realization of the utter hopelessness of solving one's problems by Level 2 methods. The path intensifies the feeling of frustration and double bind until one is like "a mosquito biting an iron bar." Concepts provide no solution. It has to arise first on a much deeper and inarticulate level. If increased philosophical clarity short-circuits this process, it would be in Buddhist terms a dubious gain.

I think that the Buddhist approach is strong enough so that we need not intellectually castrate ourselves by imitating past masters who made good teaching out of flawed logic. We need not cultivate hothouse paradoxes out of misplaced respect for Dharma. It is really the case that no one's ego style handles every situation perfectly and that no world-view explains everything. Life produces ample paradoxes because the game of ego really is hopeless. Indeed the most astonishing double binds often come from those who are trying hardest to put things with complete clarity.

1. See in particular "The Logical Categories of Learning and Communication," in *Steps to an Ecology of Mind* (New York, 1972).
2. Thomas Kuhn, *The Structure of Scientific Revolutions* (Chicago, 1962).

The I-Chou Lohan Statues and the Stages of Realization

Robert Newman

The famous tricolor ceramic lohan statues, life-size and extremely lifelike, are the most impressive remnants of the great tradition that was perhaps the most distinctive of all Chinese sculpture traditions. Though the lohan tradition became an established part of Chinese folklore, it was distinctly Buddhist in origin, based on Buddhist scriptures, Pali and Sanskrit. And the lohans created in sculpture, such as those found near I-Chou, are close to the magnificent traditions of northern Buddhist portrait sculpture characterizing Buddhist realization. The I-Chou lohans are integrally related to the training processes of monastic Ch'an (Zen) Buddhism, the meditation-practice lineage of Mahayana Buddhism. In fact, the statues are revelatory of aspects of vipassana meditation: initial realization of egoless, nondual awareness, and initial panoramic awareness.

Lohan is the Chinese translation of the Sanskrit word *arhat*, which originally (in the Pali Canon) meant "fully enlightened"; but from the Mahayana perspective, "arhat" means initial crystalization of continuous awareness, the stabilization of one's relation to stillness. In the Mahayana's use of the arhat-lohan imagery in the atmosphere of the meditation halls, the statues represent the immediate disciples of Sakyamuni Buddha — that is considered the primary representation. But they were traditionally made with realistic mixtures of Aryan and Mongolian features, more Mongolian than Aryan in the I-Chou lohans. And as disciples of the historical Buddha they were carriers of the Dharma, embodiments of its processes. So the lohans are students and teachers at once. They are teachers of the level of realization or meditation they carry. This relates these symbolic characterizations to the northern Buddhist traditions of portrait statues of living teachers, ac-

1 The British Museum, London
Photo by Betty Morris.

tualized embodiments of buddha-activity beyond the arhat stage, fuller representatives of Buddha's lineage.

The iconography of the arhat-lohans begins at Gandhara, in the famous period of the first half of the first century AD, the time of the creation of the buddha-image. In the bas relief scenes from the life of the Buddha, usually in schist stone, and on the many stupas of Gandhara, great and small, the buddha-image was often in *dhyana asana* (meditation posture). Usually he was surrounded by his arhat-monk-disciples, who were either sitting formally in meditation or not, like the I-Chou lohans. In these bas relief arhats, their shaved heads revealed bone structure in the heads and faces, and the sense of flesh in the face had the potential to express states of mind. The disciples were characterized, individually distinguished, in established ways.

In the second phase of Gandharan art, in the fourth century, the imagery produced was fully carved statuary, made for the newly developed statuary altars of Mahayana monasteries, a five-figure altar-image-complex: the central buddha-image, two bodhisattvas, and two lesser figures. This so-called pentad altar became the major altar format for Chinese Buddhism. As soon as it appeared in China, the two figures immediately beside the buddha-image were the arhat-disciples Ananda and Kasyapa, with their iconically characteristic faces.

BUDDHA

ARHAT   ARHAT

BODHISATTVA   BODHISATTVA

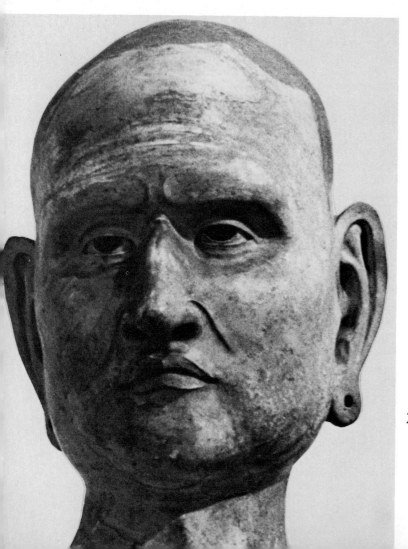

2 The Metropolitan Museum of Art, New York.
Photo by Robert Newman.

3 The Metropolitan Museum of Art, New York. Photo by Robert Newman.

Set between the highly stylized buddha-image and two stylized bodhisattvas, the portrait-character of the arhat-lohans had the potential to represent the relation between ego and egolessness in the human image. The bodhisattva and buddha images represent a progressive shift of energies from ego to egolessness. Thus the pentad altar can be said to represent three major stages of Buddhist realization, the three turnings of the Wheel of Dharma.

The powerful human ego in the power of groundlessness, or egolessness, is the situation of realized vipassana (awareness) meditation, the process developed from the practice of shamatha (mindfulness) meditation. Lohan statues, as used in the meditation halls of Ch'an Buddhism, represented the actual psychological processes of meditation that the monks in the meditation hall were engaged in. As part of the altar structure of the Buddha hall, the lohans were part of the representation of the evolutionary potential of Buddhist meditation; when the lohans were used in separate meditation halls with portrait statues of Ch'an masters (the priest portraits), they were in the same situation as in the Buddha hall. Thus there were these two possible original settings for the I-Chou lohans. A third possibility would have been a hall of their own, a lohan hall, common to later Chinese monasteries. But the I-Chou lohans have the psychological power that suggests the period of spiritual authority in Ch'an monastic training, making either the Buddha hall or other meditation hall settings more likely for these particular statues.

The pentad altar with the initial two lohans

was widely established in the great wave of creative Buddhist energy of the Northern Wei dynasty in the sixth century. The pentad altar was at the heart of the extensively excavated mountain temples and shrines as well as in the free-standing temples and monasteries. In the T'ang dynasty, from the seventh century onwards, lohans were popularly made in sets of sixteen initially, and then eighteen. The sixteen and eighteen lohan sets were often used in formal integration with the altar in the Buddha hall, extending the imagery of meditation. They were set in two rows of eight or nine statues, reaching down the sides of the hall from a bodhisattva—buddha—bodhisattva triad altar. (The whole of the statuary could be considered an extended pentad altar.) Thus the meditators were surrounded by the psychologically influential images of realized meditation. The same would be true of the separate meditation hall setting, where the meditators would be surrounded by mirror-like, realistic images of their own potential.

The I-Chou lohans were found in a cave, high on a mountain near I-Chou, Hopei province, China, in 1912, where they may have been stored for centuries, probably several times removed from their original setting. A plaque in the cave said, "All these Buddhas come from far away." Western art historians and curators have arrived at a tentative Liao-Chin dynasties dating, 10th −12th centuries. That would set them in the highly defined monastic structures of the period just beyond the last of the great Ch'an masters of the T'ang. The institutionalization of the Ch'an Mahayana teachings was firmly established by Pai Chang (720 - 814), one of the last of the great Ch'an masters. Thus the I-Chou lohans could be said to represent an effective for-malization of training to produce non-conceptual, non-referential (prajna) insight. The experience of arhat-ship represented in the images is of initial nonverbal experience, initial relation to stillness and silence, initial realization of stability and Buddha's sanity.

Of the original set of sixteen or eighteen I-Chou lohans, eight came to the West, six with their original heads, and then one of the six (a bust fragment) was lost in Germany in World War II. Of the five remaining statues with their original heads, four are in America and one is in the British Museum. In the sixty years of their presence in the various Western museums, people have had "shocking" experiences upon encountering them. To generalize from reports of such experiences, the individual coming into the presence of the lohan reaches a point of dynamic contact in which, for the moment, the statue is seen to be *alive*. A strong psychic shift or alteration of psychic functioning is produced, most often on people working in a spiritual path, frequently non-Buddhist.

As the Buddhist teachings grow dynamically in America, Buddhist meditation halls begin to materialize and the processes of meditation expressed in the I-Chou lohans begin to develop in American practicioners. In a culture which has gone to the extremes of psychological and physical materialism in a situation of hysterical insecurity, these images of monastic non-attachment, of the realization of something of Buddha's sanity, are perhaps bound to become increasingly relevant.

Clearly these statues are the work of an extraordinary artist with extensive meditation training — a master who was able to represent objectively the first great stage of realized Buddhist meditation.

4   Nelson-Atkins Gallery of Art, Kansas City.

5 The University Museum,
Philadelphia.
Photo by Robert Newman.

An Interview with Achaan Chaa

Sunno Bhikku

Achaan Chaa was born into a large and comfortable family in a rural village in the Lao area of northeast Thailand. He was ordained as a novice in early youth and at the age of twenty took higher ordination as a *bhikkhu*. Beyond a fourth grade education, which is standard in the village schools, he studied some basic Dharma and scriptures as a young monk. Later he practiced meditation under the guidance of several of the local forest teachers in the Lao-speaking ascetic tradition. He walked for a number of years in the style of an ascetic monk, sleeping under the trees and in the forest, and he spent a short but enlightening period with Achaan Mun, perhaps the most famous and powerful Thai-Lao meditation master of this century. After many years of travel and practice he returned to settle in a thick forest grove near the village of his birth. This grove was uninhabited, known as a place of cobras, tigers, and ghosts — in his words, the perfect location for a forest monk. A large monastery formed around Achaan Chaa as more and more monks, nuns, and lay people came to hear his teaching and to stay with him. Now there are disciples teaching in more than a dozen mountain and forest branch temples throughout northeast Thailand.

On entering Wat Ba Pong one is apt first to encounter monks drawing water from a well, and a sign on the path that says, "You there, be quiet, we're trying to meditate." Although there is group meditation and chanting twice a day and usually an evening talk by Achaan Chaa, the heart of the meditation is the way of life. Monks work at sewing robes and sweeping the forest paths. They follow ascetic precepts such as limiting meals to one a day and allowing themselves only a few possessions. Discipline is extremely strict, leading to a simple and harmoniously regulated community life and cutting away at the ego needs for outward display of individuality.

The author, Sunno Bhikkhu, was a monk for several years in the ascetic forest tradition. He was one of the first western disciples of Achaan Chaa. Questions in this interview were asked by him and translated from the Lao language at Wat Ba Pong monastery.

QUESTION: I'm trying very hard in my practice but I don't seem to be getting anywhere.

ACHAAN CHAA: This is very important. Don't try to get anywhere in the practice. The very desire to be free or to be enlightened will be the desire that prevents your freedom. You can try as hard as you wish, practice ardently night and day, but if it is still with the desire to achieve, you will never find peace. The energy from this desire will be cause for doubt and restlessness. No matter how long or hard you practice, wisdom will not arise from desire. So, simply let go. Watch the mind and body mindfully but don't try to achieve anything. Don't cling even to the practice or to enlightenment.

What about other methods of practice? These days there seem to be so many teachers and so many different systems of meditation that it is confusing.

It is like going into town. One can approach from the north, from the southeast, from many roads. Often these systems just differ outwardly. Whether you walk one way or another, fast or slow, if you are mindful it is all the same. There is one essential point that all good practice must eventually come to. That is not clinging. In the end all meditation systems must be let go of. Nor can one cling to the teacher. If a system leads to relinquishment, to not clinging, then it is correct practice.

You may wish to travel, to visit other teachers and try other systems. Some of you have done so already. This is a natural desire. You will find out that a thousand questions asked and knowledge of many systems will not bring you to the truth. Eventually you will get bored. You will see that only by stopping and examining your own mind can you find out what the Buddha talked about. No need to go searching outside yourself. Eventually you must return to face your own true nature. Here is where you can understand the Dhamma [Dharma].

Are the minds of Asians and Westerners different?

Basically there is no difference. Outer customs and language may appear different, but the human mind has natural characteristics that are the same for all people. Greed and hatred are the same in an eastern mind or a western mind. Suffering and the cessation of suffering are the same for all people.

Is it advisable to read a lot or study the scriptures as a part of practice?

The Dhamma of the Buddha is not found in books. If you want to really see for yourself what the Buddha was talking about, you don't need to bother with books. Watch your own mind. Examine it to see how feelings come and go, how thoughts come and go. Don't be attached to anything, just be mindful of whatever there is to see. This is the way to the truths of the Buddha. Be natural. Everything you do in your life here is a chance to practice. It is all Dhamma. When you do your chores try to be mindful. If you are emptying a spittoon or cleaning a toilet don't feel you are doing it as a favor for anyone else. There is Dhamma in emptying spittoons. Don't feel you are practicing only when sitting still cross-legged. Some of you have complained that there is not enough time to meditate. Is there enough time to breathe? This is your meditation: mindfulness, naturalness in whatever you do.

I still have very many thoughts. My mind wanders a lot even though I am trying to be mindful.

Don't worry about this. Try to keep your mind in the present. Whatever there is that arises in the mind, just watch it. Let go of it. Don't even wish to be rid of thoughts. Then the mind will reach its natural state. No discriminating between good and bad, hot and cold, fast and slow. No me and no you, no self at all. Just what there is. When you walk on alms-round, no need to do anything special. Simply walk and see what there is. No need to cling to isolation or seclusion. Wherever you are, know yourself by being natural and watching. If doubts arise, watch them come and go. It's very simple. Hold on to nothing.

It is as though you are walking down a road. Periodically you will run into obstacles. When you meet defilements just see them and just overcome them by letting go of them. Don't think about the obstacles you have passed already. Don't worry about those you have not yet seen. Stick to the present. Don't be concerned about the length of the road or about a destination. Everything is changing. Whatever you pass, do not cling to it. Eventually the mind will reach its natural balance where practice is automatic. All things will come and go of themselves.

Is it necessary to sit for very long stretches?

No, sitting for hours on end is not necessary. Some people think that the longer you can sit, the wiser you must be. I have seen chickens sit on their nests for days on end. Wisdom comes from being mindful in all postures. Your practice should begin as soon as you awaken in the morning. It should continue until you fall asleep. Don't be concerned about how long you can sit. What is important is only that you keep watchful whether you are working or sitting or going to the bathroom.

Each person has his own natural pace. Some of you will die at age fifty. Some at age sixty-five and some at age ninety. So, too, your practice will not be all identical. Don't think or worry about this. Try to be mindful and let things take their natural course. Then your mind will become quieter and quieter in any surroundings. It will become still like a clear forest pool. Then all kinds of wonderful and rare animals will come to drink at the pool. You will see clearly the nature of all things in the world. You will see many wonderful and strange things come and go. But you will be still. Problems will arise and you will see through them immediately. This is the happiness of the Buddha.

You have said that samatha and vipassana or concentration and insight are the same. Could you explain this further?

It is quite simple. Concentration (samatha) and wisdom (vipassana) work together. First the mind becomes still by holding on to a meditation object. It is quiet only while you are sitting with your eyes closed. This is samatha and eventually this samatha base is the cause for wisdom or vipassana to arise. Then the mind is still whether you sit with your eyes closed or walk around in a busy city. It's like this. Once you were a child. Now you are an adult. Are the child and the adult the same person? You can say that they are or looking at it another way you can say that they are different. In this way samatha and vipassana could also be looked at as separate. Or it is like food and feces. Food and feces could be called the same. Don't just believe what I say, do your practice and see for yourself. Nothing special is needed. If you examine how concentration and wisdom arise, you will know the truth for yourself. These days many people cling to the words. They call their practice vipassana.

Samatha is looked down on. Or they call their practice samatha. It is essential to do samatha before vipassana, they say. All this is silly. Don't bother to think about it in this way. Simply do the practice and you'll see for yourself.

I feel sleepy a great deal. It makes it hard to meditate.

There are many ways to overcome sleepiness. If you are sitting in the dark move to a lighted place. Open your eyes. Get up and wash your face, slap your face or take a bath. If you are sleepy change postures. Walk a lot. Walk backward. The fear of running into things will keep you awake. If this fails stand still, clear the mind and imagine it is full daylight. Or sit on the edge of a high cliff or deep well. You won't dare sleep. If nothing works, then just go to sleep. Lie down carefully and try to be aware until the moment you fall asleep. Then as soon as you awaken, get right up. Don't look at the clock or roll over. Start mindfulness from the moment you awaken.

If you find yourself sleepy every day, try to eat less. Examine yourself. As soon as five more spoonfuls will make you full, stop. Then take water until just properly full. Go and sit. Watch your sleepiness and your hunger. You must learn to balance your eating. As your practice goes on you will feel naturally more energetic and you will eat less. But you must adjust yourself.

Why must we do so much bowing here?

Bowing is very important. It is an outward form that is part of practice. This form should be done correctly. Bring the forehead all the way to the floor. Have elbows near knees and knees about eight inches apart. Bow slowly, mindful of your body. It is a good remedy for our conceit. We should bow often. When you bow three times you can keep in mind the qualities of the Buddha, Dhamma and Sangha. That is, the qualities of mind of purity, radiance and peace. So we use the outward form to train ourselves. Body and mind become harmonious. Don't make the mistake of watching how others bow. If the young novices are sloppy or the aged monks appear unmindful, this is not for you to judge. People can be difficult to train. Some learn fast but others learn slowly. Judging others will only increase your pride. Watch yourself instead. Bow often, get rid of your pride.

Those who have really become harmonious with the Dhamma get far beyond outward form. Everything they do is a way of bowing. Walking,

they bow; eating, they bow; defecating, they bow. This is because they have got beyond selfishness.

What is the biggest problem of your new disciples?

Opinions. Views and ideas about all things. About themselves, about practice, about the teachings of the Buddha. Many of those who come here have a high rank in the community. They are wealthy merchants or college graduates, teachers and government officials. Their minds are filled with opinions about things. They are too clever to listen to others. It is like water in a cup. If a cup is filled with dirty, stale water it is useless. Only after the old water is thrown out can the cup become useful. You must empty your minds of opinions, then you will see. Our practice goes beyond cleverness and beyond stupidity. If you think to yourself, "I am clever, I am wealthy, I am important, I understand all about Buddhism," you cover up the truth of anatta or non-self. All you will see is self, I, mine. But Buddhism is letting go of self. Voidness. Emptiness. Nirvana.

Are defilements such as greed or anger merely illusory, or are they real?

They are both. The defilements we call lust or greed or anger or delusion — these are just an outward name, appearance. Just as we can call a bowl large, small, pretty or whatever. This is not reality. It is the concept we create from craving. If we want a big bowl we call this one small. Craving causes us to discriminate. The truth, though, is merely what is. Look at it this way. Are you a man? You can say yes. This is the appearance of things. But really you are only a combination of elements or a group of changing aggregates. If the mind is free it does not discriminate. No big and small, no you and me. There is nothing. Anatta, we say, or non-self. Really, in the end there is neither atta nor anatta.

Could you explain a little more about karma?

Karma is action. Karma is clinging. Body, speech or mind all make karma when we cling. We make habits. These can make us suffer in the future. This is the fruit of our clinging, of our past defilement. All attachment leads to making karma. Suppose you were a thief before you became a monk. You stole, you made others unhappy, made your parents unhappy. Now you are a monk but when you remember how you made others unhappy you feel bad and suffer yourself even today. Remember that not only body, but speech and mental action can make conditions for future results. If you did some act of kindness in the past and remember it today, you will be happy. This happy state of mind is a result of past karma. All things are conditioned by cause — both long term and when examined moment to moment. But you need not bother to think about past, or present, or future. Merely watch the body and mind. You must figure karma out for yourself. Watch your mind, practice and you will see clearly. Make sure, however, that you leave the karma of others to them. Don't watch others. If I take poison, I suffer. No need for you to share it with me! Take what is good that your teacher offers. Then you can become peaceful, your mind will become like that of your teacher. If you will examine it you will see. Even if now you don't understand, when you practice it will become clear. You will know by yourself. This is called practicing the Dhamma.

When we were young our parents used to discipline us and get angry. Really they wanted to help us. You must see it over the long term. Parents and teachers criticize us and we get upset. Later on we can see why they do so. After long practice you will know. Those who are too clever leave after a short time. They never learn. You must get rid of your cleverness. If you think yourself better than others you will only suffer. What a pity. No need to get upset. Just watch.

Would you review some of the main points of our discussion?

You must examine yourself. Know who you are. Know your body and mind by simply watching. In sitting, in sleeping, in eating, know your limits. Use wisdom. The practice is not to try to achieve anything. Just be mindful of what is. Our whole meditation is looking directly at the mind. You will see suffering, its cause and its end. But you must have patience. Much patience and endurance. Gradually you will learn. The Buddha taught his disciples to stay with their teachers for at least five years. You must learn the values of giving, of patience and of devotion.

Don't practice too strictly. Don't get caught up with outward form. Watching others is bad practice. Simply be natural and watch that. Our monk's discipline and monastic rules are very important. They create a simple and harmonious environment. Use them well. But remember the esscence of a monk's discipline is watching intention. Examining the mind. You must have wisdom. Don't discriminate. Would you get upset at a small tree in the forest for not being tall and straight like some of the others? This is silly. Don't judge other people. There are all varieties. No need to carry the burden of wishing to change them all.

So, be patient. Practice morality. Live simply and be natural. Watch the mind. This is our practice. It will lead you to unselfishness. To peace.

Brushwork by Jackson C. Hollomon

The Future (if any) of Tantrism

Agehananda Bharati

Photo courtesy of Syracuse University News Bureau

The topic of this talk is Buddhist and Hindu Tantra, but it is not on what Tantrics *ought* to do or what they *ought* to read or what they *ought* to meditate about, but what they actually *do* do and what they *may do* if in the future they survive, which is the big question. I am talking here not as a Tantric, not as a monk, but as an anthropologist, as a person who talks *about* religion rather than talking religion. If you analyze a religion you can do it in at least two ways — you can do it normatively, that's what a priest does, that's what a Rinpoche does, that's what a convert does, that's what people do in order to inspire each other, in order to understand what the religion means *for them*. But that's very different from asking yourself the other question, "What is the practice and what do the practitioners of a particular cult or religion do, what do they actually do in this world, how do they communicate with others, how do they stand, what

is it, what is their function in society, and what can be done with, to, or from them?"

As I said, talking *about* religion is something quite different from *talking* religion, very much like talking *about* emotion is not emotional. You see, the term "emotion" is not an emotional term, it's a *descriptive* term. Therefore, when you talk about emotion as a psychologist or as a behavioral scientist, you don't talk emotionally unless this happens by chance to be your style. So when I talk about Tantrism I'm not talking about what the kundalini does inside of you or outside of you, but about what people who think the kundalini does something, what *they* do to each other, or what they may do, etc. What H. V. Guenther talked to you about, or Rinpoche himself, all this *is* the Tantric tradition, it is talking about Tantra *as* Tantrics should hear about Tantra. These are instruction manuals, either oral or written, about what to do, but they are not about what *you* do, what you as Tantrics *are*. I have to assume that you are aware of the basic Tantric teachings. My question therefore is, what does Tantra do by way of operating inside society? Is there such a thing as Tantrism as an "institution," in the anthropological sense? Are there Tantrics? That sounds like a silly question but it's not a silly question at all because there is doubt as to whether there ever were any Tantrics. Religious people *say* certain things, believe they do them, when they don't. Now, the anthropologist listens to him, to the practitioner, whether he is a religious or economic or magical practitioner, to what he says. But he also observes whether the person actually does what he says.

I remember many years ago I heard that in the mountains in India there was a great young yogi who levitated about two yards into the air. I said, "This I have to see," so I snuck my Leica under my robe and went up to the place where this young saint was supposed to levitate. There we were sitting on mats, and he was sitting on a mat, and we started chanting, simple chants, and that went on the whole night, and in the morning they asked me, "Well, wasn't it great?" I said, "What, what?" They said, "Didn't you see him levitate?" I said, "No." "Oh," they said, "that's because you're not initiated." The verb "to levitate" does not mean that a person levitates, but that people *say* he levitates. That's what it means. When I say this guy's got a green jacket, I actually say that about the green jacket. When I say that girl over there is pretty, grammatically it sounds like the same structure, but it isn't, because I don't say anything about her at all. I say something about my state of mind, which I hope, vaguely, others will share or not share, as the case may be. These are not descriptive terms, they are *emotional* terms, or they are *persuasive* terms. So the term "levitate" is a persuasive verb. It does not describe the act of levitation, but it describes the state of mind of the people who believe that someone levitates. Now these are all very important preambles when you talk about religious behavior, *actual* behavior, not *normative* behavior, not like Christian missionaries talking about Christianity as it ought to be, or as they think it is in the Bible, but how Christians *act*.

Another way of putting this is that you have two different ways of analyzing any kind of cultural behavior. We are talking about Tantric behavior here. One way of analyzing it is the way the Tantric himself analyzes it, for his fellow Tantrics. This is called the *emic* way. The *emic* way of stating things is talking about things and acting about things in a way that makes sense to the co-agents of the culture in question, to the people who share the same language, culture, world-view, whatever it is. But it does not necessarily make sense to the critical observer. Now the critical observation which makes sense to *other* critical observers on a cognitive level — that is called the *etic* strategy. So first I'm going to give you an *emic* definition of Tantrism, and then I'm going to give you the *etic* definition of Tantrism.

An analogy: if somebody says, "God has one son and his name is Jesus," that is an *emic* statement of a believer in certain forms of Christianity. How could you translate it into an *etic* statement? I did it just now. The *etic* statement is, "There are certain people in the Christian religion who say and believe, 'God has one son and his name is Jesus.'" End of *etic* statement. That is a statement of facts as they are. Now let us talk a bit about our beloved kundalini. She is a very graceful lady coiled up in dark nether regions at first, but hopefully rising up to light, higher regions. When you talk about the kundalini as though she existed, that is *emic* talk. When you talk about what Tantrics say and write about kundalini, that is *etic* talk. When an anthropologist talks about Tantrics and says, "Tantrics are yogis who manipulate a mental construct which they think has some kind of existential status and which they refer to as 'The Coiled One,' Kundalini," that is *etic* talk. Another way of putting this is to say that doctrinally Tantra is a radical interpretation of the salvational complexes including doctrines and *sadhanas* (exercises), shortcutting the more tedious and time-consuming ones of orthodox yoga, utilizing the sensuous equipment of the mind and body of the practitioner rather than eliminating it. That would be an *emic* statement, made by an articulate Tantric when asked for a definition. The *etic* statement would run like this: Tantrics are groups of more or less organized meditational practitioners who use, or say they use, esoteric ritual, including elements not acceptable to the official dominant religious traditions of the countries they originated in, aiming at the liberation from the doctrinally postulated cycle of *samsara*, of birth and death.

This takes us to a much wider anthropological definition of religion: "Religion or magic (which is the same thing) is the manipulation of culturally postulated extra-human entities." That's all there is to any religion ever practiced. All the entities are "culturally postulated," whether they are Jesus Christ or the *atman* or *shunya* or *Chenrezi*. These are culturally postulated entities or non-entities — which means culturally postulated things or names — and they are manipulated systematically. This is an *etic* definition of religion, and probably the most comprehensive, in our present state of knowledge. So that in order to want to do Buddhist yoga or Tantra, you have to postulate, "Everything is misery." *Etically*, that's a matter of taste. Americans who espouse Asian religious teachings think that rebirth is somehow *nice*. But if you think rebirth is nice, you should do something else. Because the object of Tantra is the termination of rebirth — to crack the wheel of existence. Even in the case of those Mahayana doctrines which declare the total identity of *samsara* and *nirvana*, if you observe this kind of doctrinal speech carefully, you will notice that this identity is one with considerable strings attached: for though by this doctrine everybody really is a *bodhisattva*, the implication is that everybody really *is not*.

We now assume *etically* that the focal activity of antiestablishmentarian Tantrism did indeed include at one time some kind of arcane sex or some kind of ritualistic usage of other "ingredients" which were not acceptable to the cultural body surrounding the Tantrics. Assuming this is the case, then we would have to assume further that there are indeed Hindu or Buddhist Tantrics, or there were such people, and this is a very tough problem. In other words, were there Tantrics, or were there just people who engaged in sexual congress using mantras along with it? Now we know there are people who copulate. There must be some. We also know there are some people who use mantras. I am quite sure I know a number of people who use sex and mantras at the same time. Do they actually do Tantrism? Well, as a behavioral scientist, you must say yes, for obviously that's what they do. Whether there is something deeper to it or not, that of course is outside the focus of any possible sociological-anthropological analysis — it takes us into the abyss of what's called phenomenology, one of the intellectual aberrations of this century.

How does Tantrism work, or does it work, or how could it work? First, it cannot now nor ever again work in India. Next, it cannot work in Tibet because there is no Tibet. The majority of those Tibetans who could work it out live in an environment that won't tolerate it — that is, in India. The degree of hostility, embarrassment, dislike, distrust between Tibetans and Indians is so complete that you can't really even talk about it. Don't forget that when Tibetan Buddhists talk about *Jagar*, that is not the India of today with rupees and pennies and Mrs. Gandhi, and curry and intolerable amounts of heat. It is the *Jagar* of the texts, the India of the first spread, where Buddhist teachings first happened in this cycle. It is a bit like theosophists talking about the Himalayas. They are not talking about the Himalayas which were climbed by Tenzing and Hillary, but some mysterious range sheltering a sacred brotherhood dressed in white and floating through the air on magic carpets and what-not. But these Himalayas do not exist. The ideal and the actual Himalayas are something very different. So when Tibetan scholars, monks and laity, who are engaged Buddhists, talk about Buddhist India, they don't talk about *this* India, which they dislike.

Lastly, where can Tantra happen? It can only happen in America and Western Europe. There is no possible framework for it in Eastern Europe. Tantrism may happen here and maybe it has started right here in Boulder, Colorado 80302.

If Tantrism is to establish itself, it cannot do so in India because India is not what it used to be. India is perhaps the most puritanical country in the world. Sex is sin, whether it is marital sex, extramarital sex, any sex. I always tell my students before they go to India, "Don't confuse India with Khajuraho and the erotic sculptures. That was nine hundred years ago. When Mahatma Gandhi was asked about this artistic genre, he said, and I quote, 'If I had the power, I would pull them down.'" Antisexual puritanism is axiomatic and there's no way out. If Ram Dass and some others who have been there for a very short time tell you that deep down all this *is* there, either they are not informed or they are not telling the truth. But since I give them the benefit of the doubt, I say they are just not informed.

Let me start the rather longish list of caveats, of warnings, of what Tibetan Buddhism and Tantrism cannot be, or should not be in this country, one of the few in the world where it could take root and flourish. First of all, although I hold an American passport and I vote, since I was not born here I can say there is one cultural disease in this country, and that is what I call *hypertrophical eclecticism*. To give you an example, in a record store the other day, I saw an LP named "Aloha Amigo." This is all wrong. Deep down, many of you think it is nice. But it isn't. It's either "aloha" *or* "amigo." Now, just because something is different from Mommy and Daddy, and different from Richard Nixon and Billy Graham, that alone doesn't make it good. Just because it has an Indian accent doesn't make it good. There have to be other criteria. The trouble here is that anything that's different from home is put together and looks like something real. Unfortunately, in a very refined and sophisticated manner, this tendency is even represented in what I saw in your program print-out here. Weaving and karate and T'ai Ch'i don't have to appear together just because they are Asian. There is a tradition, there is a rule, there is a lineage that you must be able to trace. But *sitar and tabla and saxopone and escargot and tatami* — that's just *Aloha-Amigo*. I don't think it leads anywhere.

I once asked Ravi Shankar how well George Harrison played the sitar. So Ravi thought for a while and said, "Well, he holds it quite well." This dismal eclecticism in America is largely representative of the counter culture. Ted Roszak's *Making of the Counter Culture* was an important book, but he missed this point. The reason why LSD-droppers and yogis and leftists got together was because of that pan-American eclecticism. Nobody these days listens to a Wagnerian opera which lasts five hours, but people listen to a potpourri, "The Best Of . . ." "The Best of Mozart," "The Best of Duke Ellington," you name it. There *is* no "The Best Of." You have to hear the whole work. That's at the back of meditational discipline — you have to go right through it by one of its techniques. It's extremely boring, but if you won't do it, I can only say: there are other kicks. They cannot be found in any serious tradition which requires assiduous, patient, non-eclectic individual application.

If you make the mistake, and I hope you don't, to believe that what you have here is *the* answer to the world's problems, you are exactly on a level with Guru Maharaj, or Hare Krishna, *I Ching*, T'ai Ch'i Ch'uan, or Billy Graham and Jehovah's Witnesses, except that your diction is more sophisticated. But the degree of conviction doesn't mean anything about the world. It only means that there are different degrees of conviction as psychological factors in some individuals.

Now those of you who haven't heard of this lecture of mine, or read about it, please fasten your seatbelts. Or as Margaret Rutherford said in the movies, "I didn't *bring* any seatbelts." I'm coming to a very important *etic* statement which has to be taken to heart by anybody who does any kind of meditation, Tantric or non-Tantric. And that is the simple but unpleasant fact concerning yogis and mystics and saints and prophets so far: *the mystical experience does not confer ontological status upon its content*. In other words, from the fact that someone sees God, or Chenrezi, it does not follow that Chenrezi or God exists. It only follows that given certain conditions, certain people are sure that they have seen God, or Chenrezi, or the Angel Gabriel, etc. The very important difference between the mystic and the prophet is this: the mystic (the word derives from the Greek *myesthai*, to shut up) has an incomparable, unique, irrefutable personal experience — but it does not bother him at all whether or not his experience implies the existence of the divinity, godhead, etc. *outside* the experience. In contrast to the mystic, the prophet insists that because he has seen or heard God (or some other superhuman agency), He exists apart from his experience. Mystics are harmless people, prophets are dangerous. They see something and they think because they've seen it, it exists, and other people have to accept it, or else they are damned. But the trouble is that although you experience all sorts of lovely things, Heruka embracing Heramba, Amitabha sitting on the head of Avalokiteshvara, etc., it doesn't mean that these divinities exist. The fact that you do it all along the kundalini doesn't mean that the kundalini exists, it only means that these are important crutches for certain meditations. Now some Mahayana teachings say just that: the great founding father of Madhyamika Buddhism, Nagarjuna, was asked, "Well, sir, you are destroying all propositions of your opponents. What are your own propositions?" He answered, "There are no propositions. The only real proposition for a true Buddhist is to dismantle all propositions." Mystical experience has no ontological content; those who claim it does may be good mystics, but they are lousy philosophers. Since we have eaten from the tree of empirical knowledge, prophetic skills do not work.

As I already told you, you have to learn to think about things both *emically* and *etically* but not during the same time of the day. You have to create an artificial schizophrenia, as it were, between the *emic* and the *etic*, and you must not be fazed by psychiatric terms, all of which are words of reprimand or abuse. The terms used in the clinical terminology of the psychiatrist and psychologist are not descriptive terms, although practitioners think they are. The terms "schizophrenic," "paranoid-schiz" and so forth are not descriptive terms like TB or malaria, but they are terms in the minds of the fraternity called psychiatrists. The term "schizophrenic" means you don't *like* the patient's behavior. The terms you learn in the course of studying a religious doctrine operate analogously. They say nothing about the universe, they say nothing about the human mind, but they think they say something that may be therapeutic. They help you achieve a certain state of mind if indeed you want to achieve this state of mind. And this has to be enough. If you feel this is counter-inspirational, and if you then insist, "But it *is*, I know the truth," you belong to the wide genre of the Billy Grahams and the Adolf Hitlers.

There are three things which Tantrism is not. It is not humanistic. It does not solve any social problems. It is not a solution to the sexual problem, or to questions about human intimacy. When I studied Tantrism years ago in India I thought that it would be the solution to my sexual problem, which was quite acute, as it is with all young monks. But it wasn't. If a great guru, a compassionate teacher, a Vajra-master, teaches you about human tenderness and about ethical behavior, these were *not* generated by his meditation, but by cool rational thinking, which has nothing to do with meditation. So please get rid of the notion that any religious practice helps you morally. Morality and religion are generically unconnected with each other. The pervasive notion that they are derives from ancient historical error, as old as India and Israel and China. In the ancient days when the great

religions of the world were founded, there were no specialists. Anybody who taught religion also taught medicine, ethics, law and everything else. There was nobody else to talk about these things. But the knowledge of how to act ethically in society cannot follow from a religious idea or any set of meditations. Although it seems self-evident to most people engaged in religion that there is a connection, there is none. The "connection" is purely accidental. We know some very, very great yogis who are impossible human beings. And we know some very fine human beings who despise yoga as totally ridiculous. The two are simply not related to each other. So please as of this moment disabuse yourselves of the notion that by doing yoga you will be a better human being. You won't. To be a better human being you have to think better. There's no other answer. To be moral means to be rational.

Coming back to the sexual question, what I see here is that most of you unfortunately, whether you admit it or not, believe that the sexual element in Tantra is somehow *nice* and *romantic* and lovely and full of nice, warm love-making. Nonsense. The sex of Tantra is hard-hitting, object-using, manipulative ritual without any consideration for the person involved. If you have such considerations, it's very good, but it has nothing to do with Tantrism. The notion that Tantrics have some privileged information about the essence of male and female *a la* Jung is nonsense. If you want to be lovers, you have to go to other sources. Predominantly yourself. There *is* other literature about it. There is Indian literature, also translated into Tibetan, but it is not found in the Buddhist and Tantric texts, it is found in the *Alamkara sastra*, the texts on *poetics*, not in the *Kama Sutra*, which is a social analysis of whores and their patrons, who were brahmins, princes, and other leisurely people of the day.

Let me conclude this. What you have to do, since we have a great teacher here, Rinpoche, who is deeply involved in a profound tradition, is to *use* all this. But I would say that for worldly and social relations in human life, other sources must be consulted. He teaches you Buddhism. As far as human relations in a complex industrial society go, he can teach you that too, but he has to learn about it like anyone else. Not by dint of his being a master, but by dint of his studying American society as a sympathetic sociologist or anthropologist would.

Further Notes from Naropa
LOKATIONS

THIS LOCATION
David Joel

Mid-December in Boulder, 1974. The Gyalwa Karmapa passed through earlier — "His Holiness, His Ordinariness," as Rick Fields put it in a four word poem — having blessed us all. A few weeks ago, Rinpoche in town giving a seminar, the three month seminary and thirty day *dathun* at the same time emptying many of their two hundred passengers back into the community here. The scene mobile and loose, crises coming and passing so quickly they're hardly worth noticing. The post-Naropa Buddhist community seems very different from last year: that high-energy input from the summer still reverberates, there's less talk about pain and boredom now, the parties are a little less frantic, or "speedy" as they say around here. The community seems much less insulated from the social network of Boulder at large — there's more sense here, I think, of the possible doom we all face, maybe more interest in the fertility of the chaos we all know has just begun.

And projected into all that, another Naropa summer coming up after another six months, probably, of social, economic, and general all purpose planetary deterioration. How many earthlings will starve between now and then, how many tight and terrified egos in Omaha or Brighton will fracture and split in the face of the now undeniable "impermanence" of what they thought were the details of a world solid as themselves? What a time for the spreading dharma. The astronomers are beginning to talk about "White Holes", points in space that possibly are "spewing forth galaxies," and even a species as untogether as ourselves just dipped a sensor within 27,000 miles of Jupiter. All that has something to do with space awareness, it seems.

But back to this location. Boulder sparkles. Lots of good movies for a buck on CU campus, lots of people here into mime and music and theatre. Naropa flourishes, which is to say survives. All those protection cords! Newcomers to the scene, many of whom stayed after last summer, seem sort of dazed, but they keep sitting. Many contributors to Loka around — Joshua Zim, John Morrow, Robert Newman, Rick Fields, Sara Vogeler, Ives Waldo, Victoria Thompson, Jeremy Hayward (just left for Karme Choling in Vermont), Jim Burbank, Rich Greene, Sidney Goldfarb, Andrew Karr. Huge Karma Dzong Christmas Crafts Fair happening. The Loka staff currently pasting up the pages you're reading. . . .

Ferrigno, Fields, Ross, Joel

NAROPA: FIRST WEEK
Victoria Thompson

Sitting around the pool at our apartment complex, playing with my child and watching/feeling the delicate social dance. On the surface — good clean fun. Splashing in the water, sunning, chatting. Pick up on the tension. See the eyes that meet only in glances. Sense the fierceness with which we hold our images in place. Cool, hip, nonchalant, pleasant, kind — however we choose to think of ourselves. The air sings with self-consciousness. Yet we're the folks that paid cash money to come see a man tell us we don't exist. . . .

Early in the morning, walking with my baby we saw a young man— — obviously blind — standing on the sidewalk. He heard us coming half a block away, smiled and cried out, "Hello." The baby went up to him, gave him a pebble. The blind man groped to find the child, ran his hands over the little legs, took him in his arms, nuzzled and hugged him, rubbed his fat belly, and put him down again. All this done with such intensity, such concentrated tenderness that, had the man had sight, I would have been inclined to look away. . .

Sitting in the meditation hall, finding it difficult to keep from staring at the beautiful Japanese monk seated at the front of the room. Rocklike in his stillness, a stone buddha, the folds of his robe bear witness to his enlightenment. Sensing perhaps the pressure of my gaze, his eyes take light. He shoots me a glance. *And it goes home.* Like an arrow, like a knife, his look enters me. What is this mystery? What does it mean for one emptiness to touch another?

Walking up to Rinpoche's evening lecture, seeing a woman I know from home. Both she and I look away. Though we care about each other, know each other well, we look away. Why? She once spent an evening with my husband. There is always a reason, always an excuse. . .

It's hard to be graceful here at Naropa, where the flame of the teaching burns so hot. We're pulled by the longing, the hunger, the nectar of knowledge so near at hand. Opposing is the fear, the embarassment, the impulse to cover ourselves any way we can. Add to this the old high school impulse to blend into the scene as thoroughly as possible, to know the hierarchy, the honchos, whom to imitate, whom to court. . . the situation becomes so confusing that it threatens to cave in on itself.

Perhaps Naropa is the place where we can just go ahead and let the apocalypse happen. Like that blind man, sing out a greeting to the darkness. Open up, invite it in.

A ROMAN CATHOLIC PERSPECTIVE
Bro. John Doyle

. . . What I sense here at Naropa is people saying ''No!'' to apathy. The ''No,'' however, is not enough. What is vital is the discovery and creation of a dimension of meaning that will enable the person to become aware of self-deception. This discovery is the first step in the realization of one's power to move beyond. ''Move beyond'' is a purposely vague phrase. What it means to a Buddhist, a Hindu, a Christian or a Jewish person is not primary. What is primary is awakening. I feel a deep sense of yearning in so many of the people studying here for such an awakening. And while Naropa may not be the cause of such awakening, for many it is the place where it has occurred. This discovery has set these people on the path of creating a new perspective for their lives. As a Christian, I have no doubt that this is the grace of God at work — that these people have allowed themselves to be touched by the mystery of God's action.

To me, the yearning and the awakening are very closely related to the spirit of Naropa — the ''spirit that cannot be denied.'' It doesn't bother

me at all that Naropa's primary concern is the Buddhist tradition. The spirit of Naropa is genuine, and all things genuine are the vehicles of truth. D.T. Suzuki said (in an introduction to *A Flower Does Not Talk,* by Zenkei Shibayama): ''Let us not forget Zen always aspires to make us directly see into Reality itself so that we can say along with Meister Eckhart, 'Christ is born every minute in my soul' or 'God's Isness is my Isness.' Let us keep this in our minds as we endeavor to understand Zen.'' Given the purpose of Zen, ''to make us see directly into Reality itself,'' then Christians and Buddhists must be prepared to recognize that, while methods and approaches are very different, perhaps the ''Reality,'' the ''Isness,'' is not so different at all.

Has there been controversy? Yes. I would have been disappointed if there were not. Honest controversy is a real source of enlightenment. That Naropa has provided the opportunity for such controversy is truly significant because it is realistic. Why realistic? Because growth and struggle go together.

In conclusion, I offer these words of Nikos Kazantzakis in *Report to Greco:*
And I said to the almond tree:
    'Sister, speak to me of God.'
And the almond tree blossomed.

SHUNYATA:
A Lognostic Gloss
George Quasha

In the best ''spirit of reversals,'' Buddhism says ''Nothing'' where anyone else would say ''Everything.'' Consider the important Mahayana term *Shunyata,* which comes to us meaning Voidness or Emptiness. At its root it evidently carries the sense of *swollenness,* which paradoxically is a kind of ''fullness.'' So how, then, is it Empty? I offer a Lognostic gloss: The fruit swells into itself out of the condition of seed, then ''collapses'' to its original condition of seed. As such, the swelling is the *same* as the emptiness from which it came — expansion and contraction, two ends of the one cyclic process. In *Man or Matter,* Ernst Lehrs, discussing Goethe's *Metamorphosis of Plants,* defines a principle of *renunciation* in life process by reference to ''flowering'': ''While progres-

sing from leaf to flower the plant undergoes a decisive ebb in its vitality. Compared with the leaf, the flower is a dying organ. This dying, however, is of a kind we may aptly call a *dying into being.*'' The plant literally cuts off its juice at the calyx, so that the ''swelling'' occurs in *reverse* of its normal life-activity: ''After achieving its masterpiece in the flower, the plant once more goes through a process of withdrawal, this time into the tiny organs of fertilization. After fertilization, the fruit begins to ·*swell. . .* This is followed by a final and extreme contraction in the forming of the seed inside the fruit. . . nothing seems to remain but a small, insignificant speck of organized matter. Yet this tiny, inconspicuous thing bears in it the power of bringing forth a whole new plant.'' This ''renunciation'' (or what Thomas Altizer, in his study of Blake, refers to as *Kenosis,* ''self-emptying'') is a sort of *transmutation by self-reversal.* Its process of self-regulation and self-extension involves a principle of self-interference.

Is *Shunyata* — the word itself — the embodiment of its own meaning? When Freud read an early work on ''The Antithetical Sense of Primary Words,'' claiming that the oldest words contain opposite meanings, he discovered the operative principle of *The Interpretation of Dreams,* the ''identity of opposites'' that resonates with Giordano Bruno's *Coincidentia oppositorum.* Herbert Guenther in *The Tantric View of Life* radically redefines Sunyata as *Openness,* reversing what to the Western mind is the frightening notion of Emptiness. He insists on the *positive* meaning of the word, much as Goethe, in his *Theory of Colors,* argued that darkness is not the ''absence of light'' but a vital reality in active dialectic with light. ''Nothingness'' is non-encumbrance, spaciousness, seed-space.

Mahamudra, the ''Great Symbol,'' gives the sense of wide open space. And space is what we ought to be ready for in America, descending from those who came here under the flag of ''More room!'' As Olson said it, thinking of Melville: ''I take SPACE to be the central fact to man born in America, from Folsom cave to now. I spell it large because it comes large here. Large, and without mercy.'' Sunyata

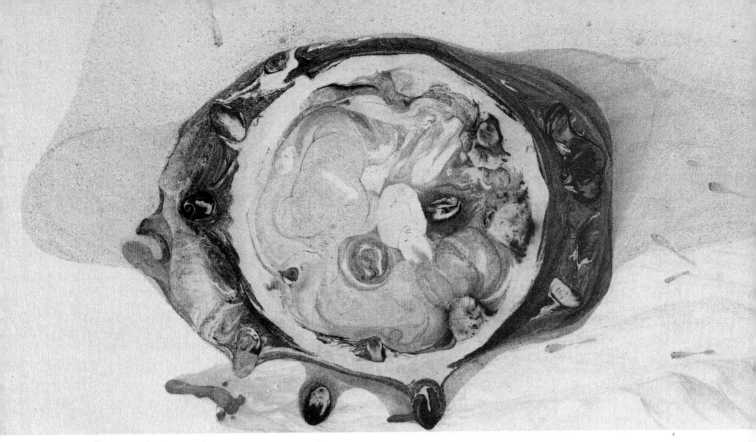

Illustration by Eugene Gregan

as Agora — and that we continue to suffer from what might be called "spiritual agoraphobia" is the cruelest of ironies.

I once mentioned to Herbert Guenther that I'd had a dream in which Sunyata came to me as a woman, and he said: "But she IS a woman!" The Occidental disease is *Sophiaphobia*, whence the Taboo against Knowing. We persist in confusing Her with the work of Satan, misreading that story about the (swollen!) fruit. But Satan, as Blake said, is *Limit;* the "Limit of Opacity," outer edge of our resistance to Light. Woman, on the other hand, is Trans- [Tara = "to cross over"] -Lucence, and as Blake says, "there is no Limit of Translucence." Or in the poet Robert Kelly's phrase, Satan is the name a person gives when he mistakes the invitation to open himself as the command to suicide.

In my dream Shunyata came showing Her hands, that She holds nothing and yet isn't exactly empty-handed, since She still has — Her hands. If we *must* see Limit in Her, perhaps we should call it the *Limit of Nothing.*

Note: The Word "Lognostic," from *"Lognosis," combines "Logos" and "Gnosis," root principles of Word and Knowing, and suggests a fundamental marriage of West and East, of Western Esotericism and Buddhism; in this way it relates to another useful combinatory term, Logodharma (Logos + Dharma).*

DOING THE DHARMA
In Super 8 & 16mm
Enid Goldstein

The film class meeting in the basement might be in the midst of discussing Hawks or Bergman, "corn" as an aesthetic, or how to deal with actors who can't act, but eventually the class gets back to *space*, a word formerly used only by real estate people, science fiction writers, or NASA. Now it is the dominant theme in Johanna Demetrakas' class, *Space and Communication in Filmmaking.*

As she talks about her work, the concept of space begins to emerge as a peaceful ozone in which energy and movement can flow or not, unhampered by directives from management, ego, or even the cosmos:

"Space comes from meditation and meditation is a way to free energy that would ordinarily go into manipulating, protecting, and justifying the ego. When you don't have to do that, you can use that energy to be open to what's around. You can see in a new way; you can work with the unexpected.

"As I've done my work, the questions I ask myself have changed. My idea of being a filmmaker has evolved into what I call the totally vulnerable dictator. That is, if you're vulnerable, you're open, you work with what's happening. You walk that tightrope between rigidity and sticking with your central vision — following your intuition, having the guts to make the decisions and take the risks that give film its great vitality, energy, even originality.

"Without ego, the subject matter can burst forth its own energy. The real teaching is that you can allow things to be what they are. You begin to accept your own faults, energy, whatever, and therefore, of course, you begin to accept other people.

"That's what this class is about— — having the space to relate to the subject without pre-conceived ideas."

Photo by Tom Raper

EXPLORING FEMININE/MASCULINE: The Way of Space and Energy
Miriam Tarcov Argulles

To think in terms of feminine and masculine immediately presents problems with built-in difficulties and challenges. We are faced with the responsibility of cutting through our own biases and fears, and must be willing to work with ourselves from the ground up.

One of the first questions we may ask before working with the masculine and feminine principles is whether this work will actually help in clarifying our situation, or whether it will maintain and prolong divisions that produce confusion and dichotomies. A fundamental challenge arises: what kind of space, if any, are we allowing ourselves as we explore the feminine and masculine? Will we tenaciously cling to the belief that there are certain definite masculine and feminine principles? Will we be unwilling to let go of them when they do not work or no longer serve any purpose other than maintaining the status quo?

In order to move and play with an inspiration, an idea, or a situation, we need a space which is as open and uncorrupted by our dualistic confusions as possible. It is a space that simply by its existence nourishes and allows a constant uncovering of ideas and intuitions accomodating the inspiration, creation, abandonment, and destruction of creative acts. Along with this basic ground of space, there is energy — an energy of origination which cannot be classified and whose source cannot be found. It is a vital spark, initiating the emergence and transformation of living matter.

TRANSFORMATION
Jose Arguelles

The present world transformation is a revolution in the truest sense of the word: to turn again, to turn back, to turn over. To these three meanings are corresponding levels of transformation: the development of mindfulness, the rebirth of traditional thought, and the destruction of outmoded forms. Mindfulness is the individual assumption of responsibility for one's own destiny, inseparable from that of the planet. The rebirth of traditional thought is the return to basic principles, uncluttered by centuries of orthodoxy. The destruction of outmoded forms is the inevitable result of centuries of injustice. These three levels interpenetrate and happen simultaneously. For many, transformation can only be a painful and disillusioning experience. Yet as a greater number of individuals assume responsibility, they will realize the necessity of returning to basic principles governing human life and expressed as the core of every world tradition. From this experience will develop new social forms and the regeneration of the principle of natural hierarchy on a global level. Natural hierarchy is the human implementation of the simple fact that the world is formally organized in an intricate chain of levels, running from the simplest to the most complex, and that planetary responsibility resides in those whose consciousness has developed to a full realization of this fact. Human society can only be a reflection of the truth of natural hierarchy, and corruption results only when the principle of upward mobility becomes exclusive, denying the validity and simultaneous necessity of downward mobility as a true balance of power.

"WHAT DO YOU REALLY NEED TO LEARN TIBETAN?"
Diane Ames

An aspiring language student once asked Chogyam Trungpa, "Rinpoche, what do you really need to learn Tibetan?" He replied, "A new mind."

As a second term Tibetan language student at Naropa Institute, I can testify: that about sums it up. Speakers of Tibetan not only have a different language, they have a different mentality. Consider their attitude about what information needs to go into a sentence. Suppose an English-speaking Tibetan wanted to translate a simple sentence like, "Sonam saw the dog near the house," into Tibetan.

For one thing, you wouldn't just write or utter a word for "dog" in Tibetan. You have to specify the social status of the dog. You would also have to know the social status of the owner of the house. And you would also have to know the social status of Sonam before you could write either his name or the verb. And you would have to know if you're quoting a speaker who's talking about his own dog, house, or relative, in which case he would have to use "non-honorific" words in referring to them. Other more or less delicate questions might influence wording, such as whether or not Sonam is a child; or whether the speaker is talking to his best friend, or whether he happens to be talking to the Dalai Lama . . . I do not fully understand the system yet. What I do understand is that there are at least two different words — an honorific word and a non-honorific word — for practically everything. I say "at least two" because the Lhasa dialect (which goes a bit overboard about the whole thing, according to non-Lhasans) has up to six different levels of honorifics. All of which means that you have to learn two or more parallel vocabularies and then consult an etiquette book.

Then there are the joys of Tibetan grammer. It's arguable that there really aren't any verbs in Tibetan, only a bunch of rather peculiar participles. One Western expert talks about "the so-called Tibetan verb." Verbs have a way of changing into nouns; and nouns transform themselves into adjectives, like so many grammatical chameleons.

The Tibetan sentence, which is often several hundred words long, is held together by bits of grammatical baling wire called postpositions. These are supposed to serve about the same function as our prepositions — that is, explaining the relationship of words and phrases to one another in terms of time, space, and so on. That's what they are supposed to do. But it turns out that these postpositions have so many different possible meanings that you wonder whether they're really put there to explain anything or to gradually undermine the reader's sanity. For example, suppose we have a relatively simple looking phrase:

ང་ནང་དུ་སོང་བ་ཡས་

The words turn out to mean "I-indoors-into-went," and then there's the postposition ཡས . So you look it up in Jaeschke's *Grammar* and it says that its three most likely meanings in this context are *a. just before, b. while,* or *c. after.* So this hitherto innocent looking phrase should be translated "just before I went indoors," or "while I was going indoors," or "after I went indoors." You put these three possibilities in a hat and pull one out.

Actually the idea seems to be that you deduce the exact meaning from context like Sherlock Holmes (who, I am convinced, must have loved the language he encountered during his famous trip to Tibet), or you conclude that if the speaker didn't care about making things clear, why should you?

Tibetan grammar and syntax, formidable as they are, are not the only problems that confront the student. There simply aren't enough Tibetan language materials — grammar books, textbooks, dictionaries, and so on — available in English. If you set out to acquire any, you will inevitably run into one of four typical problems:

(1) You need an elementary Tibetan textbook. You can't believe that there is none, not on literary Tibetan anyway. But there isn't.

(2) There is a grammar that is supposed to be quite good. But it was published in India in 1902 by the Foursquare Fundamentalist Missionary Press. It has been out of print ever since. The last copy on the market was eaten four years ago by tropical bookworms in a backstreet warehouse in Calcutta.

(3) There is one decent Tibetan-English dictionary, Sarat Chandra Das' *A Tibetan-English Dictionary;* and it is in print, but only in India. Just when you are about to start studying Tibetan, you discover that the Naropa Institute library has just bought up all nine of the copies in this country.

(4) At last someone tells you that the University of Washington puts out an elementary text on colloquial Tibetan. You send for it and then discover that its Tibetan passages are not written in Tibetan. They're written in an arcane transcription that nobody without a degree in linguistics could be expected to read.

Should you finally get hold of a copy of the Chandra Das *Dictionary* you discover that it leaves something to be desired. A lot of words and idioms are not listed, and Das' understanding of Buddhist concepts is often downright woeful. So you look up the Tibetan word for "dakini" — and the dictionary says it's a kind of Tibetan witch. Or you try to look up the main verb that unlocks the meaning of a 150 word sentence and the dictionary either lists nothing that could possibly be helpful or else the only meaning it gives is "yak manure." And so you throw the dictionary out the window.

Or you conclude that the word you were trying to look up was probably misspelled in the first place. The student's final frustration is that you can never reasonably assume that what is printed on the page is what is theoretically supposed to be there. In two years of desultory study of Tibetan, I have never seen a single Tibetan text that was not riddled with spelling mistakes.

Then there are the grammatical mistakes. There's the puzzling fact that while most American students distinguish the instrumental case from the genitive case, many Tibetan writers do not. And so on. Geshe Wangchuk told his Tibetan Four class at Naropa, "Grammar is not that important in Tibetan because it's all mistakes anyway." The class managed a bit of strained laughter, and went back to acquiring a new mind.

MAITRI PROJECT:
Space Awareness Training
Marvin Casper

"*Maitri* could be translated as love, or as a kind, friendly attitude. In this case, a friendly attitude means that making friends with someone is accepting their neurosis as well as their sanity. *Maitri* is an all encompassing friendship that relates with the creativity as well as the destructiveness of nature. But the first step is trust in ourselves. Such trust can only come about when there is no categorizing, no judgments, but a simple and direct relationship with our being."

— Chogyam Trungpa, Rinpoche

The Maitri Project began as an application of Tibetan Buddhist psychology and meditation practice to the problem of mental disorder. It was initiated by Chogyam Trungpa, Rinpoche. The Maitri program consists of meditatively relating to daily domestic situations in a communal environment and using the technique of Space Awareness, a technique created by Trungpa as a substitute for sitting meditation for highly disoriented people. The staff of Maitri found that the Space Awareness practice was a powerful meditative experience for them as well. Consequently, Trungpa has decided to offer the practice to students through residential training programs sponsored by Naropa Institute at the Maitri facility in Connecticut.

The discipline of Space Awareness involves maintaining postures within specially shaped and colored rooms for a lengthy period of time. Attention is focused on the space in the room. Each posture and room is designed to evoke a different style of relating to space. These styles, which contain both sane and neurotic aspects, are classified in terms of the "Buddha families" — karma, padma, ratna, buddha, vajra. According to Tibetan Buddhist Tantra, the Buddha families are fundamental patterns of energy which manifest in all phenomenal experience. Brief descriptions of the karma and padma styles of relating to space and the postures and rooms associated with them will illustrate how the Space Awareness practice works.

Karma involves rapid movement from place to place. Action is efficient and quick, without hesitation or impulsiveness. It is the family of the athlete, the soldier, the activist, the organizer. Karma thrusts aggressively toward an object, so it is symbolized by a sword and the wind. The thrust is narrow, long and penetrating. Karma is very direct in its approach; it touches forcefully, manipulates and passes on. It destroys and creates. It moves so rapidly that it attends to a huge number of details.

The dominant characteristic of the neurotic aspect of karma is paranoia. The world seems highly dangerous. We attack space and guard against rebounds; we live in a world of enemies who must be defeated or contained. The more afraid we become of this threatening world, the more dangerous it becomes. Loss of confidence leads to our holding back or acting too soon. We become afraid of change and try to control situations by speedily running about; and our speed may become so hysterical or blind that we lose contact. We may seem very busy but accomplish little.

The karma room, which is completely green, has a small square floor with a high ceiling containing a large square window. Karma posture is lying flat on the back, hands close to the sides, the legs spread partially apart. The window high above invites a narrow, long movement upward. However, there is nothing to touch but the endless sky, nowhere to move but

the same route again and again. We feel vulnerable to the space coming back at us. The positive potential in this posture is that we give up the struggle to defend ourselves by jumping about and realize that we can move about freely; space does not attack us and we need not attack space.

Padma is communicating with others by acknowledging their uniqueness and separateness and then

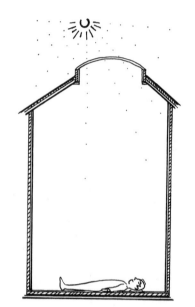

Maitri Room for Karma Posture

uniting or merging with them. We open to the presence of our partner and warmth is shared. It is a soft, receptive relationship with the world. Padma has a very refined sense of discrimination, a sensitivity to aesthetics and nuances of feelings.

In Padma neurosis there is a sense of incompleteness. The more we panic about losing the presence of our partner, the more we struggle to hold on, to possess. This passion closes us to genuine communication. We develop our own version of our partner — our ideal — about which we become more and more dogmatic. In padma neurosis we seek entertainment all the time. We try to draw things toward us, to magnetize what is valuable. Easily seduced, we are hyper-sensitive to the lure of colorful energy. Our attention is drawn to the surface of things. There

is a tendency to be highly ingratiating and acutely sensitive to rejection or coldness.

Padma posture is lying on the side, one arm extended out fully and the other resting on the hip. The room is red and square with large windows on two walls. The room suggests a seductive environment and the posture invites entertainment. But nothing passes by, nothing entertaining happens, our seductive gestures are futile. The positive potential is that we may discover an already existing presence to which nothing need be added.

The postures create a sense of frustration or vulnerability in relation to the psychological spaces suggested by the rooms. The high level of irritation and defensiveness that is provoked and sustained by this practice challenges our adjustment to the world. The disruption of our defenses is important because we usually don't see our defenses as such. We get stuck in them. We take our paranoid view of the world and our defensive response as "reality." In Space Awareness practice our response to the unchanging and objectively safe rooms is so exaggerated that we may realize that our shifting perceptions of the room are our own creation. This insight may allow us to relax our struggle with space sufficiently to realize that from moment to moment we are faced with the alternative of letting go, of opening to a saner, more balanced relationship to the world, or panicking and intensifying the struggle to manipulate it.

As the Space Awareness practice carries over into the everyday life of the Maitri community, students see their own and others' neuroses being magnified. These neurotic impulses are neither repressed nor indulged, rather they are acknowledged without being encouraged. The idea is not to feed neurotic games but allow and support exploration of them. An atmopshere of acceptance and friendliness is combined with a firm resistance to being seduced. Since students do all five postures, they develop an appreciation for the dynamics of neuroses other than their own. This encourages empathy and understanding in relating to others — one might even say *maitri*, loving kindness.

SPACED IN
Anne Jurika

Does Naropa really have an ending? As I sit here on a mountainside in the Colorado wilderness that question doesn't seem strange. About two miles back on the trail I stood and looked around, trying to take in the immensity of the view. "Seeing, seeing," I repeated like a good Buddhist mindfulness student, but finally gave in to the feeling that it was impossible to open wide enough to grasp the magnificence of the views spread out before me in every direction. So I continued on my way, content to see an aspen tree here, a waterfall there, consoling myself with the thought that later on, back home, I could draw the imprints of the mountains out of my mind like a polaroid picture.

But I knew that was no compensation for the feeling of missing so much in the here and now. If only I could wake up and be totally here! Suddenly an image flashed through my mind of the *Collaborations in Space* class, and I heard a familiar voice saying, "Focus on the space! Focus on the space!" Instantly boulders snapped into place, wildflowers were distinct from the corners of my eyes, and mountains stood in sharp three dimensional vision against close-ups of pines and distant clouds and blue sky. Space, the common factor, filled the valley from the ranges near Aspen all the way to Conundrum Hot Springs above the timberline. Space contained it all — the river, the trees, the mountains — and me, united with everything by this shared emptiness. I began to see everything as it was in space. Looking at a flower, I saw how space cut in around its petals. I heard how space narrowed between me and the sound of a cricket that I was approaching. I noticed that there was less space on the parts of the trail which ran through dense forests and more space when I walked along the side of a steep cliff. Despite my ego's pretensions I could not ignore the obvious fact that I had no more claim to this space than anything else. Realizing that I was feeling a lot of love and fulfillment, I knew that I was experiencing the "spaciousness" that Rinpoche had talked about so much — when I looked at things I was

"allowing them space" to be, rather than trying to grasp and hold on to them, or rejecting them. It was as if Naropa had planted seeds in me, and now the sprouts which had grown in my darkness all summer were suddenly blossoming, prodded by direct confrontation with reality.

AN INTERVIEW WITH THICH THIEN-AN

This interview took place at the Boulderado Hotel, the day after Dr. Thich Thien-An's public talk at Naropa on "One Mind."

Loka: Could you tell us something about Vietnamese Buddhism?

Thich Thien-An: Vietnamese Buddhism can be understood through geography. Vietnam is between the North and South. South is India, Burma, Thailand, Laos, Cambodia. North is China, Japan, and Korea. Vietnamese Buddhism has mostly developed as nonsectarian Buddhism. We take some parts from Theravadan concepts, like the *Vinaya*, and other parts from Mahayana, like the bodhisattva idea in Zen Buddhism. Therefore the Buddhist Association in Vietnam is formed from both groups.

Do each keep the separate teachings?

Yes, they have different temples, different groups, different monasteries, but when we work together, they work together. My master is a tantric Buddhist, from the *Ma-ton* school, which originally came from China. He does a lot for the hungry ghosts, *pretas*, and he does a lot of mantra and mudra. I myself am interested in Zen meditation. However, I do mudra and mantra too, because that is one aspect of Buddhism.

It seems there is a strong karmic link between America and Vietnam. How have Vietnamese Buddhists met the political situation?

In Buddhism we try not to be too involved in political situations. However, in Vietnam the majority of the people are Buddhists. So whether we are involved or not involved we are still involved in the national activity. In 1963 the government arrested many Buddhist professors, monks and nuns. They arrested me and put me in

jail for two months without reason, because I am a Buddhist. So we formed activity against that policy.

Then another point is this: the American government listened to the propaganda of the Vietnamese gov-

Dr. Thich Thien-An

ernment, and they believed that Buddhists are all communists. But Buddhists can never become communists. Do you know why? Because communists are anti-religion. But Buddhists don't like corruption in government, therefore they try to do something to stop that corruption.

Many Americans wonder why Buddhist monks immolated themselves.

About twenty thousand Buddhist monks, nuns, and professors were in jail. They were arrested by the government and nobody knew. That was an emergency case. I was released from jail by those monks who died, because when those monks burned themselves, then newspapers, magazines, and television and also the United Nations sent an investigation delegation to Vietnam, and I was released from jail one night before the delegation arrived. It is like the Christian martyrs. But in Vietnam it is more meaningful, because only seven monks dying released and saved almost twenty thousand people from jail. In Vietnam we consider the first monk to do that a bodhisattva because he died for his religion and to help us. At that time, if no one had done that, then all of us would have died in jail and nobody would have known.

In Buddhism the first important precept is not killing, not killing oneself and not killing others. But in such an emergency there was no other way to help. They were using their bodies like a lamp for help. And it was help. You know, at midnight they moved me from this jail to another, they covered my eyes, and many times I thought, this is my last chance, they are going to kill me. Nobody knew. People here did not know. People in the world did not know. After this kind of dying people paid attention. We got help from that. That is a bodhisattva. But in regular conditions it should not be done. We don't need that help now. When everybody was in jail nobody could do anything at all, except some sacrifice like that.

Can you tell us something about the social activities of Buddhists in Vietnam?

In each village and in each province we have a Buddhist high school, called Bodhi High School, which is working very well. Then in 1964, I and two Buddhist monks formed a Buddhist University which now has about seven thousand students. There are many different departments — Buddhist study, Zen study, literature, sociology, economics. Not just about Buddhism. We also have a free clinic and an orphanage. Because in this kind of war there are a lot of people injured, a lot of people suffering.

Could you say more about the bodhisattva ideal?

Bodhisattvas have an ideal, but to carry it out is very difficult. A bodhisattva vows to stay in hell until the last person gets out. But really — when is the last person? It is very difficult. New people keep coming in, so he has to continue life after life after life. Then, maybe someday, sooner or later, everybody will become enlightened, and hell will be empty.

— *Rick Fields*

DHARMA ART
Chogyam Trungpa

In talking about dharma art, we do not necessarily mean art which depicts Buddhist symbols or ideas — the Wheel of Life, the story of Gautama Buddha, etc. — but rather art which springs from a certain state of mind on the part of the artist. We can call this the meditative state: an attitude of directness and unselfconsciousness in one's creative work.

The basic problem in artistic endeavor is the tendency to split the artist from the "audience" and then try to send a message from one to the other. When this happens, art becomes exhibitionism: the person gets some tremendous flash of inspiration, then rushes to "put it down on paper" to impress or excite others; or the very deliberate artist strategizes each step of his work to produce certain effects on his viewers. No matter how well-intentioned or how technically accomplished, these approaches inevitably become somehow clumsy and aggressive, toward others and toward oneself.

In "meditative" art, the artist embodies the viewer as well as the creator as he works. Vision is not separate from operation, and there is no fear of being clumsy or failing to achieve what he aspired for: he simply makes his painting, poem, piece of music, whatever.

In this sense, a complete novice could pick up a brush and, with the right state of mind, produce a masterpiece. This is possible, but it is a very hit-and-miss approach. In art, as in life generally, we need to study our craft, develop our skills, and absorb the knowledge and insight passed down by tradition.

Whether we have the attitude of a student, who can still become more proficient in handling his materials, or the attitude of an accomplished master actually creating a work of art, there is a sense of total confidence. Our message is simply appreciating the nature of things as they are and expressing that without any struggle of hopes and fears. We give up aggression, either toward ourselves, believing that we have to make a special effort to impress people — or toward others, thinking that we can put something over on them.

Genuine art, dharma art, is simply the activity of nonaggression.

PRAJNA

Chogyam Trungpa

This summer I directed *Prajna* with Mudra, a group working with Rinpoche toward developing an American Buddhist theatre. "Prajna" is the Sanskrit word for the fundamental intelligence which sees things as they are. It is not a logic imposed on reality, but the clear perception of earth and space. The play shows a succession of people directly confronted by phenomena beyond their "understanding," phenomena that cannot be fit into the pattern of domesticated reality.

Prajna is a simple play. It must be paced so that each action is given space, so that each gesture complements and fills out the text. Our greatest problem was moving and acting with simplicity and directness — whether simply walking across the stage, lifting objects, or placing them on the altar — rather than trying to find a "right" way of doing such things.

This precision of action and gesture is particularly important for the men and women in maroon robes, who serve as uncompromising spokesmen for the teachings. Their behavior cuts through the neurotic trips of the people they confront; their actions arise spontaneously without reference to passion, aggression, or confusion. Their gestures become statements that are straightforward, but do not follow any predictable social pattern. There is no chance to argue or reason with them.

The play is based on "The Heart Sutra," a distillation of the voluminous *Prajnaparamita* (Perfection of Wisdom) literature, which is central to Mahayana Buddhism.

— Andrew Karr

Prajna *was first performed by the Mudra theatre group at Naropa Institute in Boulder, Colorado, on August 11, 1974.*

The play is performed in a large rectangular space with a circular performance area in the middle. Aisles lead to the circle from three points of the compass. When the audience is seated around the circle, the musicians go to their places at the fourth point of the compass. When the house lights go down, the actors go to their places in the dark.

*

A recorder duet is heard, then lights come up revealing six people dressed in white pajama-like clothing, holding brooms and facing each other at the center of the circle. They still sway to the recorder music even after it is finished. Their actions seem somewhat self-conscious and devotional. After a short time they turn outward as a group and begin sweeping the area in a choreographed pattern — out to the edge of the circle, in again, out again, and exit. Woodblocks clap.

Two men in white re-enter with a low wooden table, place it near the center of the circle, bow affectionately to each other, and exit. Another man brings on a large gong, places it on the center of the table, bows and exits. After a pause more objects are brought on: flowers, bowls of fruit, candles, incense, finally a plate of cream cheese and a basket of bagels. All exit.

From behind the audience a bugle fanfare is heard which is quickly joined by the percussionists. All parade on stage behind two large flags of India and the United States, which are placed in stands by the shrine. The music stops. They bow to each other, music recommences, and all march off. Blackout.

**

In darkness a *shakuhachi* flute is heard. The sound is penetrating. A single light picks out the shrine. Wood-blocks clap four times. Clustered in the three aisles, the company chants the entire *Heart Sutra*:

Thus have I heard: Once the Blessed One was dwelling in the royal domain of the Vulture Peak Mountain, together with a great gathering of monks and bodhisattvas. At that time the Blessed One entered the samadhi which examines the dharmas, called "profound illumination," and at the same time noble Avalokiteshvara, the bodhisattva-mahasattva, looking at the profound practice of transcendent knowledge, saw the five skandhas and their natural emptiness.

Then through the inspiration of the Buddha, Shariputra said to Avalokiteshvara: "How should those noble ones learn, who wish to follow the profound practice of transcendent knowledge?" And Avalokiteshvara answered: "Shariputra, whoever wishes to follow the profound practice of transcendent knowledge should look at it like this, seeing the five skandhas and their natural emptiness. Form is emptiness, emptiness itself is form; emptiness is no other than form, form is no other than emptiness; in the same way feeling, perception, concept and consciousness are emptiness. Thus all the dharmas are emptiness and have no characteristics. They are unborn and unceasing, they are not impure or pure, they neither decrease nor increase. Therefore since there is emptiness there is no form, no feeling, no perception, no concept, no consciousness; no eye, no ear, no nose, no tongue, no body, no mind; no appearance, no sound, no smell, no taste, no sensation, no objects of mind; no quality of sight, no quality of hearing, no quality of smelling, no quality of tasting, no quality of sensing, no quality of thought, no quality of mind-consciousness; there are no nidanas, from ignorance to old age and death, nor their wearing out; there is no suffering, no cause of suffering, no ending of suffering and no path; no wisdom, no attainment and no non-attainment. Therefore since there is no attainment, the bodhisattvas abide by means of transcendent knowledge; and since there is no obscurity of mind they have no fear, they transcend falsity and pass beyond the bounds of sorrow. All the buddhas who dwell in the past, present and future, by means of transcendent knowledge fully and clearly awaken to unsurpassed, true, complete enlightenment. Therefore the mantra of transcendent knowledge, the mantra of deep insight, the unsurpassed mantra, the unequalled mantra, the mantra which calms all suffering, should be known as truth, for there is no deception. In transcendent knowledge the mantra is proclaimed:

OM GATE GATE PARAGATE PARASAMGATE BODHI SVAHA

O Shariputra, this is how a bodhisattva-mahasattva should learn profound transcendent knowledge."

Then the Blessed One arose from that samadhi and praised the bodhisattva-mahasattva Avalokiteshvara, saying: "Good, good, O son of noble family! Profound transcendent knowledge should be practiced just as you have taught, and the tathagatas will rejoice."

When the Blessed One had said this, Shariputra and Avalokiteshvara, that whole gathering and the world with its gods, men, asuras and gandharvas, their hearts full of joy, praised the words of the Blessed One.

Lights come up on the circle. A woman wearing maroon robes walks slowly and deliberately to the shrine, kneels, removes a candle, rises, turns and walks off. A man, also in maroon, enters from another direction, removes a bowl of fruit, exits. Others enter singly or in pairs to remove objects from the shrine, until only the gong remains. One of the robed men enters in the dignified manner that characterizes all of the maroon-clad ones, and places an empty vase on the shrine. Again the *shakuhachi* is heard. After a pause a woman in long white robes, carrying a white flower, enters and walks slowly and deliberately to the shrine, kneels and places the flower in the vase. She then stands, and turning away from the shrine, speaks:

NAMO TRASA
BHAGAVATO
ARAHATO
SAMYAK
SAMBUDDHASA

NEVER CONTAMINATED
NEVER BAD
NEVER GOOD
ALL THE UNFULFILLED ARE FULFILLED
THE FULL MOON
MAGNIFICENT LOTUS POND
NEVER BAD
NEVER GOOD
YOUR COMPASSION IS BOUNDLESS
IT IS FOR THE CONFUSED ONES
AS WELL AS THE UNCONFUSED ONES
IT IS SO GOOD
YOUR GENTLE SMILE
YOUR KIND TOUCH
NEVER BAD
NEVER GOOD
OH, DAWN OF AVALOKITESHVARA!

Lights fade to black.

***

Top lights come up on a man dressed in dark loose-fitting shirt and pants. He is seated in the full-lotus position behind a large rock, his eyes closed. After several minutes he opens his eyes and examines the rock closely, exploring it with his hand. Then he speaks:

WHAT IS THIS STONE?
THIS ROCK?

THIS CONCRETE?
THIS SOLID GLACIER?
WHAT IS THIS FIXATION?
WHO?
WHAT?
WHERE?
WHEN?
WHY?
HOW?
SO STUBBORN.
SO SOLID.
IS THIS OR ISN'T THIS?
WHEN IS THE FORM?
WHAT IS THE FORM?
FEELING?
PERCEPTION?
CONCEPT?
CONSCIOUSNESS?

During the last few lines, the men and women in maroon enter carrying long wooden poles held upright before them. By the word "consciousness" they have formed in a horseshoe shape around him. As his speech ends, they lower their poles to point straight at him. The circle is flooded with light and wood-blocks sound.

A drum begins to beat as the pole-bearers slowly raise their poles to the vertical. They step rapidly backwards as temple-blocks sound, forward again as a bell sounds, and then lower their poles to the ground. Each time the pole-bearers raise their poles, the man lifts his rock, at first with great effort. This raising of the poles and the rock is repeated five times identically, except that each time the rock seems to have become lighter. The last time, the man lifts the rock high above his head with one hand.

Finally, the man sits on the rock as the pole-bearers recite:

FORM IS EMPTINESS, EMPTINESS ITSELF IS FORM; EMPTINESS IS NO OTHER THAN FORM, FORM IS NO OTHER THAN EMPTINESS; IN THE SAME WAY, FEELING, PERCEPTION, CONCEPT, AND CONSCIOUSNESS ARE EMPTINESS.

Blackout. All exit, including the rock.

****

The recorder players and percussionists strike up another fanfare. Lights come up as four men in red and gold enter carrying a large red blanket held at the corners high above their heads. They march ceremoniously to the center of the circle, stop, then lower the blanket to the ground. They smooth it carefully and exit.

A very ragged fisherman enters, very much out of breath. He carries a burlap sack over one shoulder and rings a cowbell with his free hand. He speaks in a brogue as he makes his way down the aisle:

BLESSINGS TO EVERYONE!
BONJOUR!
BUENOS DIAS!
GOOD MORNING!
GOOD AFTERNOON!
GOOD EVENING!
LADIES AND GENTLEMEN.

He sits down heavily on a corner of the blanket, panting and swaying. After partially catching his breath, he continues:

WELL, IT HAS BEEN A GOOD DAY TODAY.
SPRINGTIME!
GLORIOUS DAY!
I CAUGHT A LOT OF FISH.
SOME ARE SMALL AND SNEAKY,
SOME ARE MEDIUM AND SLIPPERY,
SOME ARE BIG AND DELICIOUS!
A GOOD DAY'S WORK. *PHEW*!

I WOULD SAY IT'S A PLEASANT DAY.
BUT THEN WHO KNOWS?

MAYBE THE LORD KNOWS—
BUT THEN WHAT DOES HE KNOW ABOUT FISHING?

(He sighs.)

THE LORD'S BUSY LIVING IN HIS CASTLE,
AND THAT'S WHAT HE KNOWS.

(During this speech, he has been undoing numerous knots in his sack. It is now finally open.)

ANYHOW, I BRUNG THESE FOR YOU.

(He takes out a small rock.)

THIS IS FOR M'SELF.

(He places it heavily on the blanket, then takes out another rock.)

THIS IS FOR M' MATHER.

(He places the rock on the blanket, then repeats the action for each of the following:)
THIS IS FOR M' FATHER.
THIS IS FOR M' WIFE.
THIS IS FOR M' HUSBAND.
THIS IS FOR M' UNCLE BEN.
THIS IS FOR M' AUNT JOAN.

OH, AND WE MUSN'T FORGET ST. PATRICK.
WE FOLK SURE DO HAVE A SHORT TEMPER AND A LONG MEMORY!

(He becomes more intense and slightly hostile as he continues:)

THIS IS FOR ME EYE.
THIS IS FOR ME EAR.
THIS IS FOR ME NOSE.
THIS IS FOR ME TONGUE.
THIS IS FOR ME BODY.
THIS IS FOR ME MIND.

During the last part of this speech, the pole-bearers have converged on him, poles held straight ahead. As he finishes, they surround him closely and chant in unison:

THUS ALL DHARMAS ARE EMPTINESS AND HAVE NO CHARACTERISTICS. THEY ARE UNBORN AND UNCEASING, THEY ARE NOT IMPURE NOR PURE, THEY NEITHER DECREASE NOR INCREASE. THEREFORE SINCE THERE IS EMPTINESS THERE IS NO FORM, NO FEELING, NO PERCEPTION, NO CONCEPT, NO CONSCIOUSNESS; NO EYE, NO EAR, NO NOSE, NO TONGUE, NO BODY, NO

MIND; NO APPEARANCE, NO SOUND, NO SMELL, NO TASTE, NO SENSATION, NO OBJECTS OF MIND; NO QUALITY OF SIGHT, NO QUALITY OF HEARING, NO QUALITY OF SMELLING, NO QUALITY OF TASTING, NO QUALITY OF SENSING, NO QUALITY OF THOUGHT, NO QUALITY OF MIND-CONSCIOUSNESS; THERE ARE NO NIDANAS, FROM IGNORANCE TO OLD AGE AND DEATH, NOR THEIR WEARING OUT; THERE IS NO SUFFERING, NO CAUSE OF SUFFERING, NO ENDING OF SUFFERING AND NO PATH; NO WISDOM, NO ATTAINMENT, AND NO NON-ATTAINMENT.

During this recitation, the woman in white robes walks to the gong, holding a striker. Two of the blanket-carriers return, reaching the blanket just as the recitation ends. Then, in rapid succession, clappers sound, the woman strikes the gong, and the two men pull the blanket out roughly from under the fisherman and rocks. The pole-bearers begin to chant:

OM GATE GATE PARAGATE PARASAMGATE BODHI SVAHA. OM GATE GATE PARAGATE PARASAMGATE BODHI SVAHA. OM GATE GATE PARAGATE PARASAMGATE BODHI SVAHA.

As they continue to chant, a drum joins in. Then the gong picks up the rhythm, the pole-bearers begin striking their poles together and start to circle around the fisherman. They gain speed and their circling becomes a dance.

At first the fisherman crawls about fearfully, trying to gather up the rocks. He abandons the rocks and starts to rise. He tries to break from the circle, hesitates, then tries again and again. Finally he stops and, for the first time, sees the dance. He raises his hands above this head and claps in time to the music, joining the dance.

Clappers sound. All stop, the lights fade to blackout. All exit.

*****

A single light rises to a soft glow revealing the *shakuhachi* player, in maroon robes, sitting on the shrine table. He plays. When he has finished, the circle lights come up a bit, and the men and women in maroon enter carrying brooms. They form a tight circle in front of the shrine.

One by one they turn and sweep in a precisely stylized manner to the edge of the playing area, where each places his broom on the floor and sits facing the audience.

Lights fade to black. The company begins to leave the hall. Houselights come up.

Photo by Bob Del Tredici

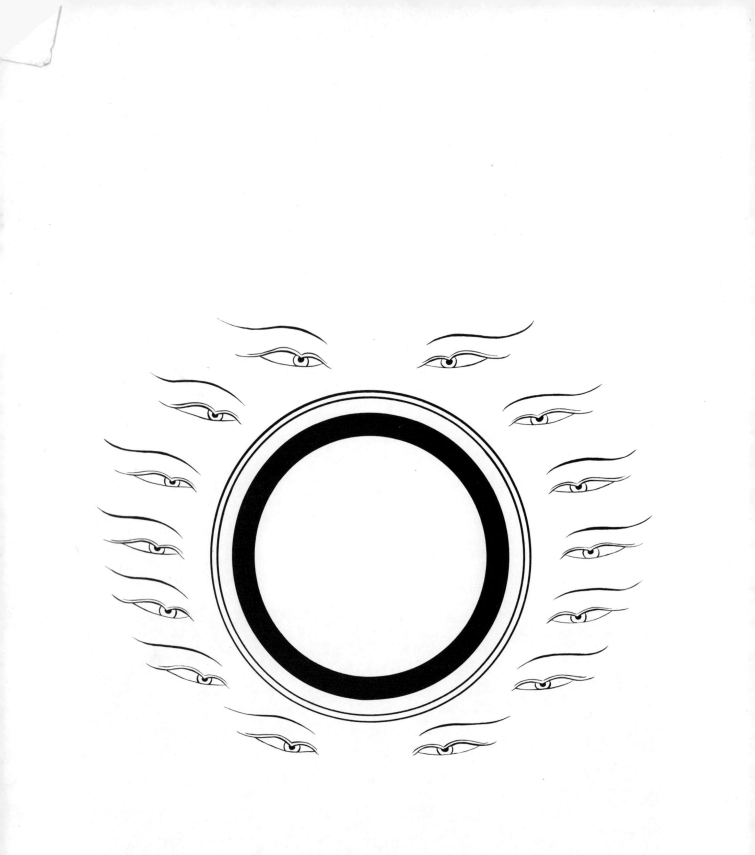